SOUTH DAKOTA

SOUTH DAKOTA BY ROAD

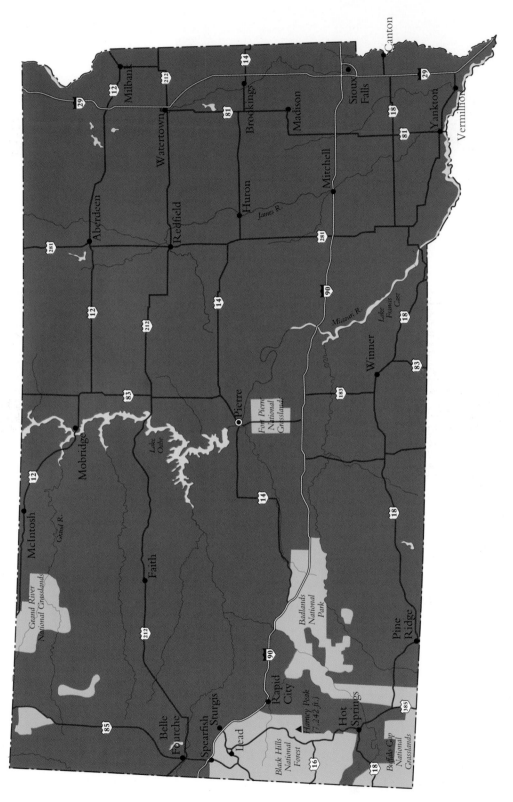

CELEBRATE THE STATES

SOUTH DAKOTA

Melissa McDaniel

BENCHMARK BOOKS

MARSHALL CAVENDISH
NEW YORK

Benchmark Books
Marshall Cavendish Corporation
99 White Plains Road
Tarrytown, New York 10591-9001

Library of Congress Cataloging-in-Publication Data
McDaniel, Melissa.
South Dakota / Melissa McDaniel.
p.   cm. — (Celebrate the states)
Includes bibliographical references (p.   ) and index.
Summary: Discusses the geographic features, history, government, people,
attractions, and highlights of this northern prairie state.
ISBN 0-7614-0419-8 (lib. bdg.)
1. South Dakota—Juvenile literature. [1. South Dakota.] I. Title. II. Series.
F651.3.M33   1998   978.3—dc21   96-49272   CIP   AC

Maps and graphics supplied by Oxford Cartographers, Oxford, England

Photo research by Ellen Barrett Dudley and Matthew J. Dudley

Cover photo: *Tom Stack & Associates*, Brian Parker

The photographs in this book are used by permission and through the courtesy of: *Tom Stack & Associates*:
Rod Planck, 6-7, 10-11; Larry Brock, 18; Charlie Palek, 24; Thomas Kitchin, 29; Peter and Ann Bosted, 112.
John W. Herbst: 13, 19, 20, 22, 64, 134. *The Image Bank*: Don Landwehrle,14; Patti McConville, 74; Marvin E.
Newman, 99; Peter Miller, 106; Jan Cobb, back cover. *Photo Researchers, Inc.*: Rod Planck, 17;
Chromosohm/Joe Sohm, 54-55; Andy Levin, 66; Margot Granitsas, 72; Ted Keras, 75; Jim Steinberg, 94-95,
103; Jan Halaska, 109; Gregory K. Scott, 117 (top); Stephan J. Krasemann, 117 (bottom); John Spragens Jr.,
119. *South Dakota Tourism*: 27, 59, 65, 67, 68-69, 77, 78 (top and bottom), 82-83, 98, 101, 104, 108-109,
115, 122, 123. *The South Dakota Art Museum Collection*: 30-31. *National Museum of American Art, Washington,
D.C./Art Resource, NY*: 33, 34. *AP/Wide World Photos*: 35, 53. *The original Dunn Painting hangs in the Hazel L.
Meyer Memorial Library, De Smet, S.D.*: 37. *The Kansas State Historical Society, Topeka, Kansas*: 39, 42. *South
Dakota State Historical Society, State Archives*: 40, 45. *Corbis-Bettmann*: 41 (top and bottom), 46, 48, 51, 90,
91, 125, 126, 127, 128, 129 (top), 130, 131. *Gamma Liaison*: Gamma, 80; S. Peterson, 85; Cynthia Johnson,
86. © *Adelheid Howe, 1983*: 88. *Rob DeWall*: 111. *South Dakota Bureau of Administration*: 116. *Animals
Animals*: Zig Leszczynski, 120. *The University of South Dakota Art Gallery*: 129 (bottom).

Printed in Italy

3   5   6   4

CONTENTS

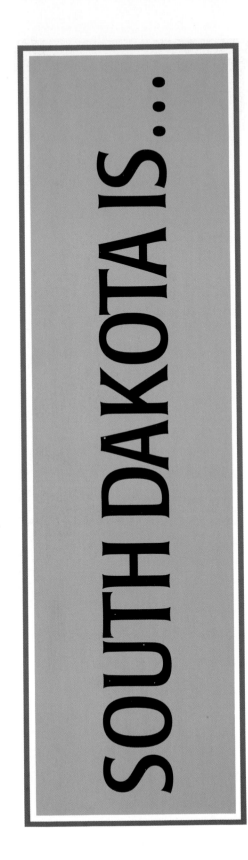

SOUTH DAKOTA IS...

South Dakota is a land of wide-open spaces.

It is "the flattest, smoothest, most treeless stretch of land imaginable. . . . When you get the feeling that the whole world can see you but no one is watching, you have come to the grasslands of North America." —Dan O'Brien, South Dakota novelist

"One notices the quiet, the near-absence of human noise."
—Kathleen Norris, South Dakota writer

It is home to hard workers.

"My father no longer wrestles a team of horses and a clumsy wagon to haul dirt. . . . Still, he works hard. . . . Hard work is a legacy of the generations who settled the prairie, broke the soil, built the sod houses, fought the droughts and grasshoppers and penny-a-pound prices for their products." —Tom Brokaw, broadcast journalist

And it is a place where people live at a slower pace.

"We treasure our world-champion slow talkers, people who speak as if God has given them only so many words to use in a lifetime, and having said them they will die."
—Kathleen Norris, South Dakota writer

Many people love South Dakota . . .

"Otherwise, why would there be so many R.V.'s roving its highways?"
—Bruce Weber, journalist

. . . but others loathe it.

"God, what a flat and empty state. You can't believe how remote and lonely it feels out in the endless fields of yellow grass. It is like the world's first drive-through sensory-deprivation chamber."
—Bill Bryson, writer

It is a . . .

"Land of infinite variety"
—state nickname

Well, perhaps not infinite. But South Dakota certainly is much more varied than people from other states think. It has magnificent mountains, eerie badlands, oddly shaped hills, and rolling plains. It is home to friendly farmers, resilient Indians, and fierce individualists—the sons and daughters of pioneers, warriors, cowboys, miners, and anyone else who wanted plenty of space between them and the next person. It is a state where history was not such a long time ago, so its echoes linger still.

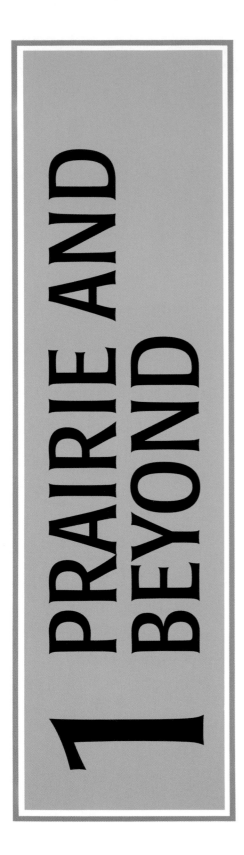

1 PRAIRIE AND BEYOND

The Missouri River runs south through the middle of South Dakota, splitting the state into two roughly equal parts known as East River and West River. The East River has more fertile land and a larger population. The West River has drier land that is more suitable to grazing than to farming; it also boasts the most notable geographic features in the state—the Black Hills and the Badlands.

EAST RIVER

When people bemoan South Dakota's flatness, they are generally talking about the East River. But even here this description is not entirely true. Ask any bicycler. After pedaling across the state, Bruce Weber concluded, "It's a myth, by the way, that South Dakota is flat. The prairie is an undulating one . . . with the road making great dips and swirls that are visible for miles in either direction. Bicycling through this is hard."

The southern part of East River country is the best agricultural land in the state, a land of gentle, rolling prairies. It is home to most of South Dakota's farms, as well as most of its people.

Farther north, the hills, while still low, are more apparent. Often nestled among them are lakes and small ponds called "prairie potholes." Some of these watering holes exist only in the spring, after the thaw and before the parched summer. Others disappear

The Missouri River, South Dakota's most important waterway, divides the state in half.

only in times of drought. They are all important to the state's animals—not to mention its people, since many make excellent swimming holes.

Moving west toward the Missouri River, the land becomes drier, the landscape browner, and the ponds fewer. Towns are farther apart. Most of this country is too dry for crops to grow. Instead, cattle and sheep graze on the scrubby grass.

Rocky buttes tower over the empty plains of northwestern South Dakota.

WEST RIVER

The West River is even less hospitable to agriculture. Just west of the Missouri, the hills become steeper and closer together. They rise one after another in strange, twisted shapes. The northwestern part of the state is flatter, except for its many huge buttes that loom over the plains. Some of these buttes are as much as six hundred feet tall. The West River gets less rain than the East River, so the land is often beige. That suits West River people just fine: "May and June are too green," says Paul Higbee. He prefers that "West River, semi-arid brown," because he doesn't have to worry about mowing the lawn.

This desolate land provides few ways to make a living. With the exception of the Black Hills, the West River is very sparsely inhabited, averaging only about five people per square mile. The population bottoms out in Harding County, in the state's north-west corner, which has less than one person per square mile. In the nineteenth century, when white settlers were still spreading over the continent, the definition of frontier was having fewer than two people per square mile. Eleven of South Dakota's sixty-six counties still fit that definition.

BADLANDS AND BLACK HILLS

Out of the prairie in the southwestern part of the state rise the Badlands, one of the strangest and most remarkable landforms in the United States. This is a rugged, desolate region of craggy ravines, eroded cliffs, and weird spires.

When the famous American architect Frank Lloyd Wright

first saw the Badlands in 1935, he had been all over the world, but nothing had prepared him for the sight. He wrote to a friend, "ethereal in color and exquisitely chiseled in endless detail, [the Badlands] began to reach to infinity spreading into the sky on every side; an endless supernatural world more spiritual than earth but created out of it."

There are many different "badlands" in the United States. The term is used for any area where water erosion has worn away soft rock and left narrow canyons and drainage creeks that are dry most of the year. In South Dakota though, the effect is particularly mesmerizing because various elements in the soil have left different-colored stripes.

These unique colors are the result of South Dakota's geologic history. Seventy million years ago, there was vast ocean over the Great Plains. It eventually disappeared, leaving a bed of black shale on which a jungle sprang up. When tree roots broke up the shale and dead plant material decomposed, the shale turned the soil bright yellow. Succeeding eras of jungle and forest and flood added new layers and colors.

About a half million years ago, the soil began to erode, exposing its different colors. This erosion has never stopped, and it is still creating a slowly changing landscape. The erosion continually unearths new fossils: remnants of clams and oysters that lived in the inland ocean, and of great tree roots that grew beside streams in lush forests— all evidence of the millions of years that went into producing the Badlands.

Although the Badlands look barren, they actually support abundant life. Rabbits, snakes, prairie dogs, meadowlarks, curlews, eagles, and even buffalo live among their shadows. Badlands National Park is home to about fifty different kinds of grasses and two hundred types of wildflowers. A single pink blossom clinging to the side of a craggy cliff is somehow more beautiful in its isolation. Juniper, yucca, wild rose, sumac, and other plants grow in the Badlands wherever the slightest bit of water is found.

The Sioux called this area mako sica, *or "bad land." Early French fur traders called it* les mauvaises terres à traverser, *or "bad lands to travel across." Today it is known as the Badlands.*

Prairie dogs live in "towns," which they make by burrowing holes and tunnels. Over time, colonies of these small creatures can move thousands of pounds of dirt in a single acre.

To the west are the Black Hills, the other outstanding landform in South Dakota. The hills were named by the Lakota Sioux, who called them *Paha Sapa*, or "Hills of Black." From afar, the slopes appear black because they are covered with dark pines. These hills contain South Dakota's highest spot, Harney Peak, which reaches 7,242 feet and is also the highest point in the United States east of the Rocky Mountains. The beauty of the Black Hills is legendary. They are renowned for their towering granite spires and magnificent canyons. In the lush forests of ponderosa pine, spruce, and

Francis Parkman, a nineteenth-century traveler, wrote that the Black Hills have "a spirit of energy and vigor . . . and they impart it to all who approach."

One of South Dakota's many outdoors enthusiasts climbs the Needle's Eye in the Black Hills.

aspen, many people enjoy walking on beds of pine needles, past gurgling creeks and stony outcroppings

In 1803, the young United States bought the Louisiana Purchase from France. This vast territory stretched from the Mississippi River to the Rocky Mountains, from New Orleans to Canada. The following year, Meriwether Lewis and William Clark headed an expedition to map the new territory and gather information about its plant and animal life, natural formations, and native inhabitants. Traveling up the Missouri River through what is now South Dakota, Lewis and Clark were overwhelmed by the immense quantity and variety of wildlife, the great herds of pronghorn antelope, elk, and bison. Although South Dakota no longer has the natural abundance it did then, it still supports a wonderful array of wildlife, particularly in the Black Hills. The state is home to white-tailed deer, mule deer, pronghorns, elk, bighorn sheep, coyote, prairie dogs, beavers, rattlesnakes, muskrats, and many other animals.

Although buffalo were hunted to near extinction in the nineteenth century, today South Dakota has over eight thousand of the shaggy beasts, more than any other state. They all live on protected reserves, on Indian reservations, or on private ranches.

For Lewis and Clark, travel up the Missouri River was slow and difficult. The muddy river's many sandbars and strong currents impeded their trip. The river that divides South Dakota today bears little resemblance to the river they saw. Four dams built during the 1950s and 1960s backed up the Missouri's water, flooding vast areas of land and creating lakes Lewis and Clark, Oahe, Francis Case, and Sharpe. These are now the state's four largest lakes and are known as the Great Lakes of South Dakota.

ON THE TRAIL WITH LEWIS AND CLARK

Lewis and Clark were awestruck by the magnificent wildlife on the Great Plains. They were particularly impressed by the pronghorns, which they called antelope. Pronghorns are the fastest animals in North America, capable of reaching speeds of sixty miles per hour. The following is from their journal entry of September 17, 1804:

This scenery already rich, pleasing and beautiful was still farther heightened by immense herds of buffalo, deer elk and antelopes which we saw in every direction feeding on the hills and plains. I do not think I exaggerate when I estimate the number of buffalo which could be comprehended at one view to amount to 3,000. . . . The antelopes which had disappeared in a steep ravine now appeared at the distance of about three miles on the side of a ridge which passed obliquely across me and extended about four miles. So soon had these antelopes gained the distance at which they had again appeared to my view I doubted at first that they were the same that I had just surprised, but my doubts soon vanished when I beheld the rapidity of their flight along the ridge before me. It appeared rather the rapid flight of birds than the motion of quadrupeds.

SUNSHINE AND BLIZZARDS

South Dakota has some of the most extreme weather anywhere in the United States. It has been called both the Sunshine State and the Blizzard State, and both names make sense. Temperatures in the state have reached as low as 58 degrees below zero and as high as 120 degrees above. Sometimes it seems as if a pleasant day of 70 degrees happens only in one's dreams. Yet South Dakotans take pride in their harsh weather. "Say what you will about our climate," South Dakota author Kathleen Norris has written. "We say it keeps the riff-raff out."

Summer days are hot, often reaching 100 degrees. The humidity is usually low, though, so it is not sticky and uncomfortable. Still, with the flatness and lack of trees, there is sometimes no escaping the bright sunshine.

Although the average yearly rainfall throughout the state is only eighteen inches, the West River often gets only twelve inches. In bad years as little as seven inches may fall, the same amount as in some desert areas. When the rain does come, it is rarely a drizzle. Instead, ferocious thunderstorms dump buckets of water, and often hail, onto the fledgling crops or parched land.

Winter can be even worse. Even without snow, the frigid temperatures can be dangerous, making even breathing painful. But it is the blizzards that are really treacherous. The blinding snow and driving wind make it impossible to do anything but sit inside and listen to the raging storms outside.

South Dakotans know how to get by. One Mobridge resident explained, "You dig yourself out, and then people usually get around alright, because everybody has four-wheel drives. Even if

A winter storm makes driving an adventure in Spearfish.

you're out on the road when a blizzard hits, you can still drive. Just open the door a crack and keep your eye on the center line." But sometimes it is impossible to drive at all. Knowing they might get stuck at some point, many South Dakotans keep a sleeping bag in their car all through the winter. They also have a shovel and a container of sand to dump on the ground for traction if they can't get moving. Some even carry a tin can and a candle, because a candle burning in a can will warm the inside of the car.

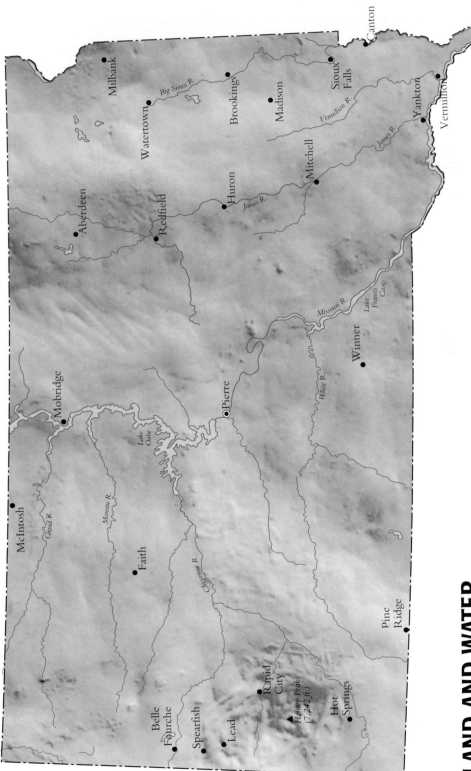

Canton

Milbank

Big Sioux R.

Brookings

Sioux
Falls

Madison

Yankton

Vermillion R.

Vermillion

Watertown

James R.

Mitchell

Aberdeen

Redfield

Huron

James R.

Lake
Francis
Case

Missouri R.

Winner

Mobridge

Pierre

White R.

Lake
Oahe

McIntosh

Grand R.

Moreau R.

Faith

Cheyenne R.

Pine
Ridge

Rapid
City

Harney Peak
(7,242 ft.)

Hot
Springs

Belle
Fourche

Spearfish

Lead

LAND AND WATER

Even the dirt in South Dakota is difficult. The West River plains have a soil called gumbo, which is a kind of clay that gets very sticky when it's wet. Walk on wet ground and you will soon find two inches of mud caked on the bottom of your shoes. It just keeps building up. And it doesn't come off when you kick your shoe against the curb. No, it stays there until it dries or until there is so much of it that it falls off from its own weight. Gumbo is particularly hazardous to people driving on dirt roads. Driving may be just fine on a gorgeous July day—until a sudden rainstorm turns the road to gumbo and traps the car.

WIND AND DUST

What really distinguishes South Dakota is the wind. No place in the lower forty-eight states is windier than the western Dakotas. With no trees or hills in the way, the air currents pick up speed as they move across the prairie. All around South Dakota, you see abandoned houses tilting precariously, a reminder of the ever-present wind.

It seems the wind never stops. It blows dust in the eyes and weathers the skin and turns walking into real exercise. And it makes the empty land noisy. Marjorie Clark, an early settler near Lemmon, wrote of the wind, "Really it is something awful and it hardly ever goes down. It actually blows the feathers off the chickens' backs. . . . I can't put up many pictures and things for every time the door opens they all blow off the wall. . . . It's so funny—we noticed how terrible loud everyone talks out here and now we find ourselves just shouting away at the top of our voices.

We discovered it must be the wind and unless you yell you can't be heard at all."

Sometimes warm winds called "chinooks" blow through the Black Hills. Howling through the mountains, these winds cause sudden, extreme changes in temperature. The largest change in temperature ever recorded in the United States came during a chinook in January 1943 in the town of Spearfish. In less than two minutes, the temperature rose 49 degrees, from 4 degrees below zero to 45 degrees above zero.

Many abandoned houses in South Dakota tilt from the persistent wind.

The constant wind makes South Dakota's periodic droughts even worse. Without moisture in the soil or plant roots to hold it in place, the dirt just blows away. On November 12, 1933, a huge windstorm moved across South Dakota, picking up dirt and tumbleweeds and gravel as it went. By the time the storm hit Sioux Falls, it was a hundred miles wide and moved at sixty miles per hour. At 11 A.M., the city became as dark as midnight. The wind smashed windows, felled telephone poles, and ripped bricks from chimneys.

This was early in the period known as the Dust Bowl, when 300 million tons of topsoil blew off the Great Plains. The price of wheat had gone up dramatically during the 1910s, so farmers had plowed more and more of the prairie grasses under. Land too dry to be good agricultural land over the long term was plowed anyway. With the grass and its roots gone, when severe drought hit in 1932, the soil just blew away. Some of the dust storms dropped dirt as far away as the Atlantic Ocean. The drought continued throughout the 1930s, and many farmers watched their land turn into desert.

Today, overcultivation of the prairie has affected the environment in other ways. Most of North America's ducks are born in the prairie pothole region of the Dakotas and Montana. The ducks rely on the small lakes and ponds to build their nests and find food. But as the prairie potholes were drained to make farmland, the numbers of ponds dropped. And fewer ponds meant fewer ducks. The 1980s saw a sharp decline in the duck population. The numbers of some types dropped by two-thirds.

In 1985, the federal government passed an act to help prevent soil erosion like that which happened during the Dust Bowl. It

Ducks thrive in the prairie pothole region, the best breeding ground for ducks in the United States.

encouraged land owners to turn farmland back into grassland, and 10 million acres were restored to a more natural state. There was also more rain than usual, so there were twice as many ponds and puddles for ducks to wallow in than there had been in previous years. In the Dakotas, this allowed the duck population to double between 1993 and 1994.

This is "probably the best opportunity to produce waterfowl on a broad-scale basis we've had since the 1950s," says biologist Jeff Nelson. "The reason is, we haven't had this extensive an area of grass with this kind of water since those days." Although the purpose of restoring the grasslands was not to help the duck population, it was a happy side effect. But the ducks are not out of danger yet, for the grasses could again be plowed under.

2 SODBUSTERS AND INDIANS

Thunderhead by Charles Greener

South Dakota's history is as colorful as its landscape is barren. Although the state was one of the last to be settled by whites, it has provided some of America's most memorable characters—outlaws and cowboys, great warriors and hardy pioneers.

THE FIRST INHABITANTS

The first people to live in South Dakota are called Paleo-Indians. They were the descendants of people who had walked on a land bridge across the Bering Strait between what are now Russia and Alaska. The oldest evidence that Paleo-Indians lived in South Dakota are campsites from about ten thousand years ago. These people were primarily hunters, living off giant bison, mammoths, sloths, and other mammals. As the climate grew drier, these large animals died off, and the Paleo-Indians turned to hunting smaller animals, fishing, and gathering roots and berries.

The Paleo-Indians were eventually replaced by the Plains Villagers, who hunted and gardened. They lived in earth lodges, which consisted of wooden frameworks with mud for walls. The Plains Villagers often lived in large towns, probably for protection. One such site, just outside present-day Mitchell, is about a thousand years old, and it is believed that as many as one thousand people lived there at a time.

THE RISE OF THE SIOUX

Eventually the tribal groups that are known today settled the area, including the Arikaras, Cheyennes, Crows, and Pawnees. In the early 1700s, the Sioux began moving onto the plains. They were pushed out of the Minnesota forests by the Chippewas, who had obtained guns from French traders. Without guns, the Sioux could not compete, so they moved west.

As the Sioux spread out across the plains, they split into subgroups. Those who stayed in western Minnesota referred to themselves as the Dakota Sioux. Those who settled in eastern

A band of Sioux required just thirty minutes to pack up their tepees and move camp. This painting by George Catlin shows them carrying their possessions on travois, sleds pulled by horses and dogs.

Native American John Lame Deer once said, "Everything we needed for life came from the buffalo's body. It was hard to say where the animal ended and the man began." Painting by George Catlin.

South Dakota became the Nakota. And those who moved west of the Missouri called themselves the Lakota.

When the Sioux moved from forest to plains, their way of life changed dramatically. They acquired horses, which they hadn't had in the forests, and they went from eating berries and small animals to surviving almost exclusively off the buffalo hunt. Buffalo pro-

WHITE BUFFALO WOMAN

Here is a story about how the Sioux came to rely on the buffalo.

One summer long ago, the Lakota people were starving because the hunters could not find any game. But then one day, far off in the distance they saw a figure approaching. It was a beautiful young woman with dark, sparkling eyes, eyes that left no doubt about the power behind them. The woman wore a glimmering white buckskin outfit embroidered with exquisite quillwork.

The woman told the Lakota that she brought something holy—the sacred pipe. She unwrapped the pipe and showed it to the people. She showed them how to smoke the pipe, what songs to sing when they filled it, and how to lift it to the sky, and then in each of the four directions.

She explained that by holding the pipe toward the sky, you become a bridge between the sacred ground and the sacred heavens. This symbolizes how everything—the earth, the sky, plants, animals, and humans—are related, are one.

When she had taught the Lakota all they needed to know, the woman walked off in the same direction from which she had come. As she walked she rolled over four times. The first time, she turned into a black buffalo. The second time, into a brown buffalo. The third time, into a red buffalo. And the fourth time, she turned into a young white female buffalo.

The moment the little white buffalo disappeared over the horizon, great herds of buffalo appeared in her place. These buffalo allowed themselves to be killed so that the Lakota would survive. And from then on, the buffalo supplied the people with everything they needed: meat for food, skins for clothing and tepees, and bones for tools. A white buffalo was the most sacred thing you could ever meet.

vided them with everything they needed. They ate the meat, made soup of the blood, and used the hides for clothing and tepees. Sinew became thread, bones made excellent tools and utensils, the tail could even be used as a fly swatter. In a few short decades, the Sioux became known as the greatest warriors, hunters, and horsemen on the plains. They were brave, fearless, generous, and honorable, and they dominated the vast grasslands.

WHITE MEN ARRIVE

Just as the Sioux were coming to power, the first European explorers entered the Dakotas. In 1743, Frenchmen François and Louis-Joseph La Vérendrye made their way to the upper Missouri River. When they returned east, they left behind a lead plate claiming the area for France; but this certainly didn't affect the area's native inhabitants.

When Lewis and Clark passed through the area in 1804, most of their encounters with the Indians were friendly. But as the nineteenth century progressed, trappers, traders, and then settlers moved into the territory, and skirmishes between Indians and whites became more common. The Indians required huge tracts of land for their buffalo hunts. To the whites, the Indians were in the way.

The newcomers knew that to get rid of the natives they had only to get rid of the buffalo. Without buffalo, the Indians would starve, and they would have no choice but to move to the reservations as the whites wanted. General Philip Sheridan prodded hunters to slaughter "until the buffalo are exterminated," because "then your

Pioneer Fanny Lyman recalled feeling "utter loneliness" as she drove "over the prairies with no path to follow. . . . There was no human habitation— only prairie and sky."

prairies can be covered with speckled cattle and the festive cowboy."

Slaughter they did. In the 1860s and 1870s, the railroads ran special trains for buffalo hunting trips. The record for a single hunter was 120 buffalo killed in just 40 minutes. Before 1800, there were an estimated 60 million buffalo on the Great Plains. By 1889, there were just 541 of these shaggy animals left in the entire United States.

THE LEGEND OF HUGH GLASS

Nearly everyone has heard of such fabled characters as Wild Bill Hickok and Calamity Jane. But another legendary character, Hugh Glass, is hardly known. He embodied the fierceness and tenacity of the trappers who were the first whites in the Dakotas.

Hugh Glass was hunting one day when he came upon a grizzly. The giant bear rushed him, and soon man and bear were wrestling on the ground. When Hugh's hunting party found him the following day, he was mauled and bleeding but still alive. The bear was dead. Hugh's companions didn't expect him to live long, with all his gashes, wounds, and broken bones. All they could do was dig his grave and wait for him to die.

After two days, the party moved on, except for two men who stayed behind to bury Hugh. They waited and waited, but Hugh lingered, unable to move, unable to speak, yet still breathing. After six days, the men decided to leave: Hugh was getting no better. Undoubtedly he would die eventually, and they didn't want to die with him.

But Hugh didn't die. Eventually he woke up. Barely able to move, he looked around. He couldn't believe his companions had left him there with no food, no weapons, nothing.

Hugh vowed revenge. He would survive. He would find those men who had left him to die. He would make them look him in the eye and explain why they had done it.

So Hugh started crawling across the desolate territory. He drank water from mud puddles. He ate berries and insects and anything else he could find. It was two hundred miles to Fort Kiowa on the Missouri River, but Hugh made it. Eventually he found the men who had deserted him. And he forgave them.

Millions of buffalo were slaughtered in the nineteenth century. Here, piles of their hides are ready to be shipped back east.

In 1868, the United States and the Sioux agreed to the Fort Laramie Treaty. This treaty established the Great Sioux Reservation, which included the Black Hills and all territory from the Missouri River in the Dakotas to the Bighorn Mountains in western Wyoming. The treaty stated that the U.S. Army would protect the Great Sioux Reservation from white settlement. But this was not to be.

THE GOLD RUSH

In 1848, Father Pierre-Jean De Smet had visited the Lakota in the Black Hills. When they showed him some gold they had found, he

United States agents and Sioux representatives agree to the Fort Laramie Treaty of 1868. The treaty established the Great Sioux Reservation, which stretched from Wyoming to the Missouri River.

told them, "put it away and show it to nobody." But inevitably the secret got out. In 1874, Lieutenant Colonel George Armstrong Custer led an expedition into the hills. Although he was supposed to be simply gathering information about the region, he was also looking for gold. And he found it. Almost immediately, headlines in a Chicago newspaper trumpeted that gold had been discovered in the Black Hills.

Miners poured into the hills, ignoring the fact that it was Sioux

Father Pierre-Jean De Smet warned the Sioux to keep the gold in the Black Hills a secret, but news eventually got out.

General George Custer was a flamboyant character prone to ignoring orders. He would lead his men where he pleased, sometimes taking along his own chef, a cast-iron stove, and a sixteen-member band.

DEAD MAN'S HAND

After gold was discovered in the Black Hills, Deadwood grew from a cluster of few shacks to a booming town of seven thousand people in just a few months. Nowhere was the Wild West wilder. The town was full of outlaws, gamblers, prospectors, and other unsavory types, and everybody was trying to make a quick buck. Into Deadwood rode and strode many of the most infamous characters in the Wild West.

Probably none was as famous as Wild Bill Hickok. Hickok had been a hunter, soldier, scout, and sheriff. But he came to Deadwood because he heard there was plenty of money to be made at the poker tables.

Some people in Deadwood were happy to see him because he had cleaned up the rough Kansas towns of Hays and Abilene. They thought maybe he could do the same thing for Deadwood. But they would be disappointed.

Not long after Hickok got to town, he made a crucial mistake. He sat in a saloon, playing poker with his back to the door. A thug named Jack McCall walked in and shot him in the back of the head. Hickok fell across the table, revealing his hand—two pairs, aces and eights— which forever would be known as the "dead man's hand."

territory. The government tried to convince the Lakota to sell the hills, but the Indians refused. They believed the Black Hills were sacred; they would never give them up. So the government began a "sell or starve" policy, trying to force them into submission. Although the treaty had said the government was to supply the Indians on the reservation with food and money, Congress cut off their rations until they agreed to give up the Black Hills.

By 1890, the Sioux had lost the Black Hills and most of their hope. On December 29 came the ultimate tragedy. Chief Big Foot and a band of about three hundred Sioux, mostly women, children, and the elderly, were surrounded by the United States Cavalry near Wounded Knee Creek, on the Pine Ridge Indian Reservation. The cavalry intended to take the warriors prisoner. Since the Indians had been traveling for weeks in the freezing winter and were cold and exhausted, they put up no struggle.

As the soldiers were disarming the Sioux, who had nothing but a few ancient rifles, a shot was fired. The cavalry then opened fire— on the warriors, on the Indians' camp, on everyone. Unarmed women and children who fled across the countryside were hunted down. When silence had returned, about two hundred Sioux lay dead on the ground, turning the snow red with blood. A few days later their bodies were buried in a mass grave. Today, above this grave a simple stone pillar lists the names of the Indians who were slaughtered at Wounded Knee.

The Wounded Knee Massacre was the last major violent confrontation between the U.S. Army and the Indians. It buried any hope that the native people could sustain their way of life. According to Patrick Cudmore, who has taught at both Harvard University and Oglala

THE DREARY BLACK HILLS

This song first appeared in print around 1875, "as sung by Dick Brown."
At the time there was no boundary between Wyoming and the Dakota
Territory, and the Black Hills belonged to the Sioux. Dick Brown was a banjo
player and singer who performed at the Melodeon, a saloon and gambling
hall in Deadwood.

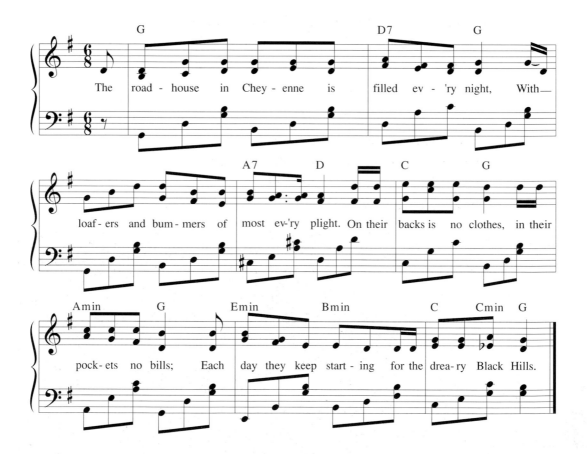

Chorus:
Don't go away, stay at home if you can,
Stay away from that city they call it Cheyenne,
Where the blue waters roll, and Comanche Bills,
They will lift up your hair, on the dreary Black Hills.

I got to Cheyenne, no gold could I find,
I thought of the lunch route I'd left far behind:
Through rain, hail, and snow, frozen plumb to the gills,
They call me the orphan of the dreary Black Hills.

Kind friend, to conclude, my advice I'll unfold,
Don't go to the Black Hills a-hunting for gold;
Railroad speculators their pockets you'll fill
By taking a trip to those dreary Black Hills.

Final chorus:
Don't go away, stay at home if you can,
Stay away from that city, they call it Cheyenne,
For old Sitting Bull or Comanche Bills
They will take off your scalp on the dreary Black Hills.

Big Foot lies dead after the Wounded Knee Massacre. A Sioux named Black Elk who recalled seeing the dead women and children said, "something else died in the bloody mud and was buried in the blizzard. A people's dream died there. It was a beautiful dream."

Lakota College, the Wounded Knee Massacre "symbolizes more than just the massacre of Chief Big Foot's ragged band, more than just the ending of America's Indian Wars and more than just the closing of America's 'last frontier.' The deeper meaning of the Wounded Knee Massacre is that it symbolized the end of almost 400 years of unrelenting war against the indigenous people of the Americas."

PROVING UP

Settlers had begun trickling into Dakota Territory after the Homestead Act was passed in 1862. The act gave 160 acres of land to anyone who built a shack on their claim and lived there for five years.

Sometimes the hardest thing about "proving up," as it was called, was just building the homestead shack. In most of South Dakota, homesteaders could look in every direction without seeing a single tree. So unless they lived next to a river, where there might be trees, log cabins were out of the question. Some people who did find wood built tar-paper-and-board shanties. But the black tar paper made them unbearably hot in the summer. And because the huts were little more than cardboard, they often just blew away in the persistent Dakota wind. Another option was the dugout, a shelter literally dug into the side of a hill, like a cave. The greatest danger with dugouts was that they sometimes collapsed.

The most popular form of homestead dwelling was the sod house, or soddy. Soddies were made by cutting large blocks of earth from the land and using them to build a house. They were superior to other kinds of shacks because they were sturdier, and they were cool in the summer and warm in the winter. But they did have their problems. Sometimes the walls leaked. Other times the floors turned to mud. And then there were the unexpected dinner guests—snakes that emerged from the walls and slithered across the ceiling.

Building living quarters was only the beginning of the battle for the homesteaders. To prove up, they had to stay on the land five years. To stay five years, their crops had to survive. But having a successful wheat or corn harvest in South Dakota is an iffy proposition any year, and doing it five years in a row practically took a miracle. If drought didn't destroy the crops, then hail would. If the

Many Dakota homesteaders lived in crude sod houses because there was no wood to build with.

summer passed without a cloud of grasshoppers descending and chewing the crops to the ground in a day, then a tornado might touch down and do the job in a few seconds. Given all this, it's not surprising that only about 40 percent of homesteaders proved up.

Still, people tried. Newspapers, railroads, and land agents lured settlers to the territory. As the railroad companies built their lines west, they established towns every few miles along the route. Where once there had been nothing but grass, towns sprang up overnight. But they left a lot to be desired. Laura Ingalls Wilder wrote of De Smet, "The town was like a sore on the beautiful, wild prairie. Old haystacks and manure piles were rotting around the stables, the backs of the stores' false fronts were rough and ugly. . . . The town smelled of staleness and dust and smoke and a fatty odor of cooking."

Even so, people came in droves to what newspapers told them was the "sole remaining paradise in the western world." Between 1870 and 1890, the population of South Dakota increased 3,000 percent. But many settlers faced bitter disappointment.

One of the hardest aspects of homesteading was the absolute isolation of life on the prairie, where the nearest neighbor might be miles away. Eliza Jane Wilder, a pioneer in eastern South Dakota, wrote in 1880, "The utter silence and loneliness grew so terrible as to be almost unendurable. I think I fathomed the depth of the word Alone." One sodbuster in ten was a woman. Some-

POPULATION GROWTH: 1870–1990

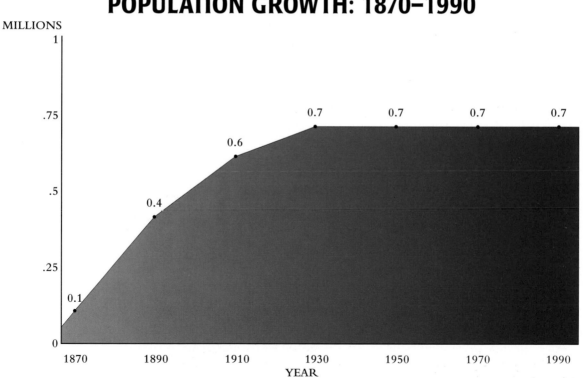

times, to ward off the devastating loneliness, sisters staked neighboring claims and worked their fields together. Occasionally they even built their homestead shacks right next to each other, one on either side of the property line.

Whether the settlers were related or not, they relied on their neighbors, both to prevent themselves from going crazy and to help them in times of need. Homesteader Edward Boyden wrote, "There are hardships to struggle with that would make strong men weak and weak men stagger. At times you got so tired you could trip sitting down. . . . It would be so much harder if it weren't for your good neighbors. . . . The only time one would spit in a neighbor's face was if his mustache was on fire."

Eventually the government realized that 160 acres was simply not enough land for survival in dry climates. So in 1909 Congress passed the Enlarged Homestead Act, which made homesteads 320 acres in states with less than fifteen inches of rain per year. But the people in charge in South Dakota didn't want potential settlers to know how dry it actually was in "the sole remaining paradise," so the state did not comply with this act until 1915.

STATEHOOD AND BEYOND

As Dakota Territory's population increased in the 1870s and 1880s, people began clamoring for statehood. In 1889 their cries were heard, and North and South Dakota were created. President Benjamin Harrison shuffled the documents admitting the two states before he signed them on November 2, 1889, so no one will ever know for sure whether South Dakota is the thirty-ninth state or

dence on the Plains   Gathering Chips.

Many women staked claims on the empty prairies. Homesteader Edith Ammons wrote of the "drab and gray and empty" land: "It would take slow, backbreaking labor, . . . to make the prairie bloom."

the fortieth. Because North Dakota comes first alphabetically, South Dakota is called the fortieth state. Although Pierre was small and out of the way, it was declared the capital because it was the town closest to the center of the state.

Life never became easy for the farmers and ranchers of South Dakota. Blizzards, grasshoppers, and drought continued to plague them. The drought of 1910–1911 was particularly bad, forcing many people off the land. While going to visit a friend seventeen miles from his home, one farmer, Oscar Micheaux, passed forty-seven houses. "Only one had an occupant," he reported. Drought was even worse in the 1930s, when dust storms blew away much of the land.

Life for South Dakota's Native Americans was harder still. For many, it was a downward spiral of poverty, alcoholism, neglect, and abuse. In the 1970s, some Sioux tried to change things. Members of a civil rights organization called the American Indian Movement (AIM) went to Pine Ridge in 1973. The reservation by this time was a miserable place. Not only were the living conditions appalling, but the tribal government was corrupt. The tribal president, Dickie Wilson, controlled a group of thugs who terrorized the residents.

In February about three hundred AIM members, Lakotas, and supporters from other tribes took over the town of Wounded Knee. They were protesting the conditions on the reservation, the breaking of the 1868 treaty, corruption in the Bureau of Indian Affairs, and the routine violence and discrimination suffered by Indians in the area. The FBI, federal marshals, and Wilson's thugs surrounded the town. The standoff lasted seventy-one days, until the government agreed to discuss the Fort Laramie Treaty with the Sioux.

In 1980, the U.S. Supreme Court ruled that the federal government had illegally taken the Black Hills from the Sioux. The Fort Laramie Treaty had stated that no changes could be made in the treaty without the written approval of 75 percent of the adult Sioux males. But the 1876 agreement in which the Sioux gave up the

Black Hills had been signed by only 10 percent. The Supreme Court concluded that the government had wanted the Black Hills gold to be mined, so it had tried to starve the Sioux and then forced a small group of them to sign the agreement. "A more ripe and rank case of dishonorable dealings will never, in all probability, be found in our history," the Court said in its ruling.

The Court awarded the Sioux more than $100 million in damages. But like their ancestors a century before, they refused the money. What they want is the land.

Members of the American Indian Movement took over the town of Wounded Knee for seventy-one days in 1973, protesting discrimination and broken treaties.

3 PUBLIC LIFE

The state capitol in Pierre

Running a society requires organization. There have to be laws that people agree upon, methods of collecting money to build roads and schools, courts to interpret how the laws should be applied, and ways for citizens to influence their world.

INSIDE GOVERNMENT

The government of South Dakota is based on its state constitution, which was adopted in 1889. South Dakota's constitution has been changed many, many times. In fact, it has been amended more than eighty times. The South Dakota constitution divides the government into three branches: executive, legislative, and judicial.

Executive. The executive branch is headed by the governor, who has many duties. Most importantly, the governor must sign any bill passed by the legislature before it can become law. Governors also focus attention on issues they think are important, call special sessions of the legislature, and appoint high-ranking officials. The governor is elected to a four-year term but may not serve more than two terms in a row.

Legislative. The legislative branch of government makes laws and passes budgets. The South Dakota legislature is made up of a thirty-five-member senate and a seventy-member house. Legislators' terms are two years, and they may serve no more than four

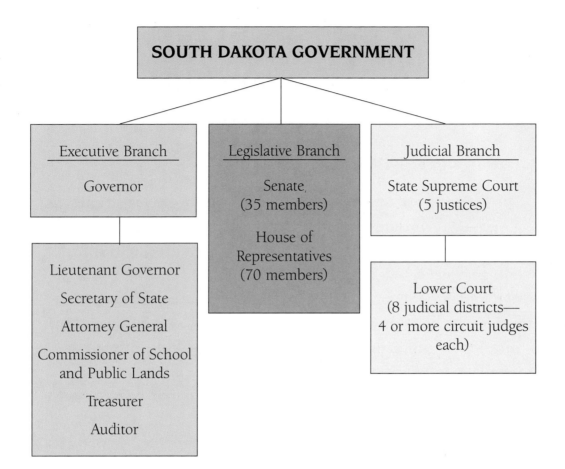

SOUTH DAKOTA GOVERNMENT

Executive Branch

Governor

Lieutenant Governor

Secretary of State

Attorney General

Commissioner of School and Public Lands

Treasurer

Auditor

Legislative Branch

Senate, (35 members)

House of Representatives (70 members)

Judicial Branch

State Supreme Court (5 justices)

Lower Court (8 judicial districts— 4 or more circuit judges each)

terms in a row. South Dakota's legislators are not professional politicians. In fact, the legislature meets for only three months annually, making the capital of Pierre a lonely place for much of the year. The rest of the time, the senators and representatives are farmers and business people, lawyers and housewives.

Judicial. South Dakota's judicial system is headed by the state supreme court. The court rules on whether laws have been applied correctly and whether new laws passed by the legislature violate the state constitution. The court consists of five justices, each appointed by the governor. Three years after the justices are appointed, the people of the state vote on whether to retain them. Thereafter, justices must by reapproved by a statewide vote every eight years.

THE PEOPLE SPEAK

The citizens of South Dakota have always been very active in governing their state. South Dakota was the first state to adopt the initiative and referendum, two methods for citizens to directly influence what laws are enacted. In an initiative, if enough people sign a petition requesting that a certain law be adopted, then it is put on the ballot in the next election. If a majority of the citizens vote for it, the ballot measure becomes law. In a referendum, people sign petitions asking that an existing law be put on the ballot for the public's approval. Then if the majority vote yes at election time, the law stands; if they vote no, it is struck down.

Having initiatives and referendums on the ballot sometimes increases people's interest in the political process, so they are more likely to vote. Some people believe this is one reason South Dakota traditionally has a very high voter turnout. In the 1994 elections, South Dakota had the highest turnout in the nation, with 60 percent of the voting-age population going to the polls, compared to only about 40 percent nationwide. More South Dakotans may vote because the state population is so small that they are likely to have met the candidates. South Dakota State University political science professor Bob Burns thinks South Dakotans vote in higher numbers also because going to the polls isn't the problem it can be in some big cities. "People don't anticipate long lines to vote," he explained, "and the polls are not far away."

In 1989, a system known as video lottery was created by the state legislature. Although it was called a lottery, it was actually gambling done on computer terminals located in gas stations, bowling alleys, restaurants, and bars. People played such games as poker and blackjack, sometimes betting hundreds of dollars in an hour. The state received about 38 percent of the money that the players lost. This revenue quickly became the fourth largest source of money for the government, after federal grants, sales tax, and

Main Street in the small town of Philip is far removed from the hustle and bustle of big-city life.

motor fuels tax. By 1994, South Dakota received $65 million per year from the eight thousand video lottery machines.

Then in August 1994, the state supreme court ruled that the video lottery was unconstitutional and ordered all the machines shut off. The South Dakota constitution permitted the state to operate a lottery but not "games of chance." Almost immediately, a constitutional amendment was drawn up to allow video lottery. It was put on the ballot in the November election.

All across the state, people argued about the video lottery. Although video lottery had been active only five years, those who favored the amendment claimed that the state could not afford to lose such a big source of money. "Our opposition has not come forth with a replacement for the money. That's too much to cut," said Lee Brown, who worked for passage of the amendment. South Dakota is one of the few states that doesn't have an income tax, and

GROSS STATE PRODUCT: $21.8 BILLION

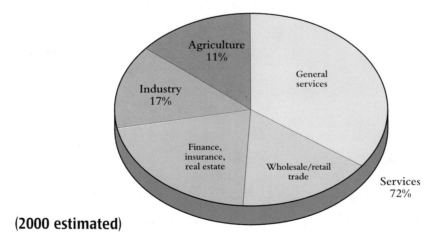

Agriculture
11%

General
services

Industry
17%

Finance,
insurance,
real estate

Wholesale/retail
trade

Services
72%

(2000 estimated)

people don't want one. Supporters of video lottery said the state might have to institute one if it lost the money from gambling.

Those against the amendment believed that video lottery was an unreliable source of income for the government, a quick fix that wouldn't solve the state's long-term economic problems. "You can't expect to gamble your way to prosperity by sitting on a bar stool gambling," said state representative Jack Billion. "Neither can the state." Others argued that many people had become addicted to playing video lottery and spent much more money than they could afford. They said that in the five years of the lottery's existence, South Dakota had seen record high numbers of divorce, suicide, and bankruptcies. Sioux Falls resident Ruth Edwards insisted that it was wrong for the state to contribute to such problems. "What next?" she asked. "How about legalizing addictive drugs and justifying it by giving the state a percentage?"

When the election finally came, the video lottery amendment passed, with 53 percent of the vote. The video lottery machines were turned back on. But many people believe the issue is not dead. Some think the video lottery would be voted down if it were put on the ballot again. "The government's become too dependent on the money," said one Mobridge woman, "and a lot of people are mad because it goes into jails instead of education like they said it was going to."

LAW AND ORDER

South Dakotans are proud of their low crime rate. In 1995, South Dakota had the third-lowest crime rate in the nation and the

EARNING A LIVING

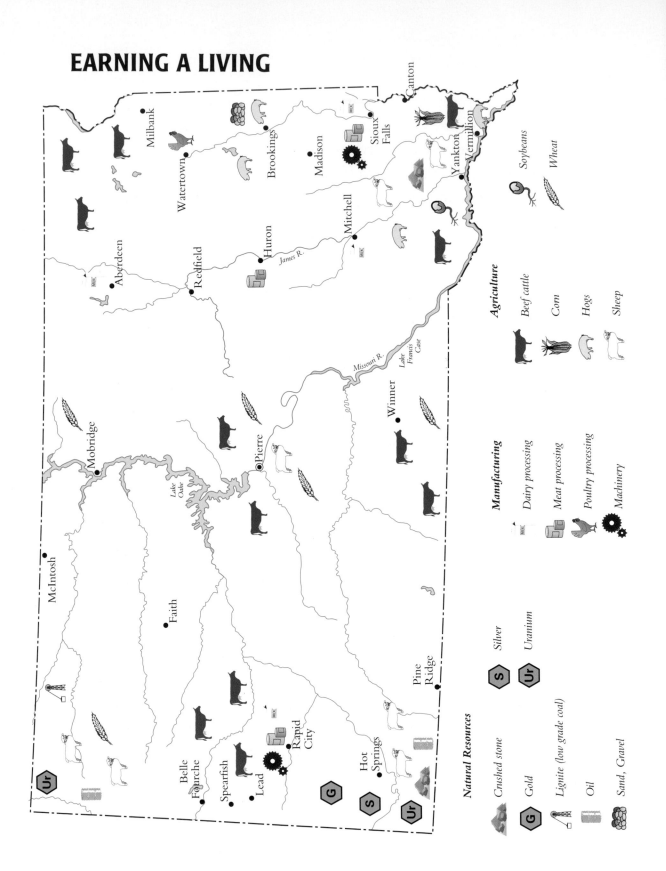

Canton
Milbank
Brookings
Sioux Falls
Madison
Vermillion
Yankton
Watertown

Soybeans
Wheat

Aberdeen
Redfield
Huron
James R.
Mitchell

Agriculture

Beef cattle

Corn

Hogs

Sheep

Missouri R.
Lake Francis Case
Winner

Mobridge
Pierre
Lake Oahe

Manufacturing

Dairy processing

Meat processing

Poultry processing

Machinery

McIntosh
Faith

Pine Ridge

Natural Resources

S *Silver*

Ur *Uranium*

G *Gold*

Belle Fourche
Spearfish
Lead
Rapid City
Hot Springs

G
S
Ur
Ur

Crushed stone

G *Gold*

Lignite (low grade coal)

Oil

Sand, Gravel

second-lowest murder rate. Many people attribute this to the state's high level of incarceration: it ranks sixth in locking criminals up. In the 1980s, in response to rising crime of the 1960s and 1970s, South Dakota began putting more people in jail. In the decade since, the crime rate has dropped. This "affirms we are on the right track," says state attorney general Mark Barnett. "Being tough on crime does hold down the crime rate."

Others disagree, pointing to nearby states such as North Dakota and Minnesota, which have, as well as low crime rates, low incarceration rates. To some, this proves that putting too many criminals in jail is a waste of money that would be better spent on things such as education. "Why are we incarcerating three times as many people as North Dakota and Minnesota?" Sioux Falls resident Dave Waldowski wondered. "If we could incarcerate as [few] as North Dakota, we could close down Springfield [jail]."

MAKING A LIVING

South Dakota has always had a boom-and-bust economy, primarily because it was based on agriculture. High prices and good weather mean prosperity for farmers, but falling prices and a drought can quickly put them out of business.

Today, agriculture remains an important part of South Dakota's economy. Farms and ranches still stretch over nine-tenths of the state. Almost half the state's population lives on farms. In 1995, South Dakota was the nation's leading producer of hay, fifth producer of oats, and eighth of soybeans and wheat. It is also a major supplier of corn, sunflowers, barley, sorghum, cattle, and hogs.

South Dakota is among the nation's leading producers of hay.

But since the farm crisis of the 1980s, when many small farmers went out of business, more and more South Dakotans are working in the financial and service industries. Tourism has become a major industry, employing one out of every twelve workers in the state. More than six million people visit South Dakota every year.

Sioux Falls, the economic center of the state, seems to have no trouble attracting new businesses. Citicorp, one of the nation's

Sioux Falls is the cultural and economic center of the state.

largest banking companies, runs its credit-card operation out of Sioux Falls. The city is also a major center for retailing, medical services, and communications, as well as a transportation hub.

This business boom means that Sioux Falls has low unemployment and relatively high wages. Elsewhere, people are not so lucky. One woman who recently moved from Sioux Falls to the small town of Spearfish, on the edge of the Black Hills, said things were much harder out there and that people often have to work two jobs just to make ends meet. "In Sioux Falls, even people working in McDonald's get six dollars an hour," she said. "But out here, it's minimum wage." Even though she had eighteen years' experience as a nurse's aid, she could only find a minimum-wage job in a Spearfish nursing home.

Things are even worse for Native Americans. Shannon County, in Pine Ridge Indian Reservation, is the poorest county in the entire nation. In 1994, 63 percent of the people on the reservation lived in poverty, compared to 14 percent nationwide. Despite such desperation, things are looking up. The casinos that have sprouted on so many reservations in the last decade have brought in much-needed cash. Many other kinds of businesses are growing on the reservations as well, including newspapers, manufacturing, and tourism.

Problems such as poverty and alcoholism continue to plague Native Americans, but many people, such as this elderly Pine Ridge woman, have endured.

Many of the impoverished residents of Pine Ridge reservation are children. Almost 20 percent of American Indians are less than ten years old, compared to about 10 percent of the rest of the U.S. population.

"A lot of things have failed out here in Indian Country," says Fred Dubray, a Sioux from the Cheyenne River reservation. "So we started to think back to the days when we were self-sufficient, back to the days of the buffalo." Dubray has built up a large herd of bison. Bison meat has become increasingly popular with American consumers because it has less fat and cholesterol than beef has. Like his ancestors, Dubray uses all parts of the buffalo. The skin becomes clothing, the bones become utensils, and the skulls are made into jewelry, which is sold in gift shops. Although Indian income has not risen much, most people believe there is more reason for hope than there has been for generations.

4 A SMALL-TOWN WORLD

In South Dakota, East River and West River are more than just geographic areas. They also define people. The East River is thought to be home to urban and conventional peoples, whereas the West River has a whole lot of rough, independent-minded folk. But many South Dakotans scoff at this alleged divide. "Nah, there's not much difference," said a woman who had moved from Sioux Falls, the heart of the East River, to distant Spearfish, in the West River. "People here have been real nice to us."

TOWNS AND NEIGHBORS

On both sides of the Missouri, South Dakota is defined by its small towns. The state's largest city, Sioux Falls, has just over 100,000 people, and the second largest, Rapid City, has about 55,000. After that, the size of towns quickly dwindles.

Most people who live in South Dakota's small towns are happy to be there. They like the quality of life, the neighborliness. "I hope we can preserve some of this," says Dennis Menke, owner of a boot store in Yankton. "That's the thing about America, we're so set on always *changing* things. Well, I'm not." Menke believes that small-town life forces people to treat each other decently. "We try to think long-term with people, give them a little extra care," he said. "You can't just scoot people in and out the door and take

TEN LARGEST CITIES

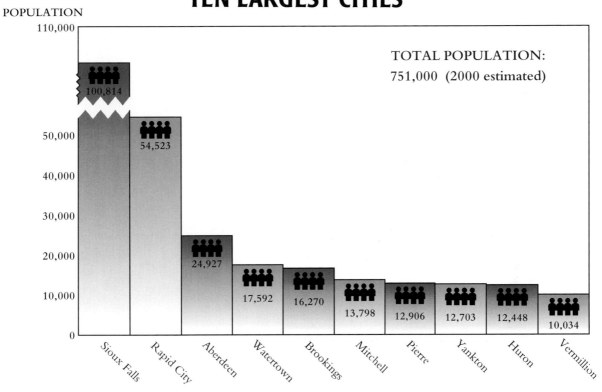

POPULATION

TOTAL POPULATION:
751,000 (2000 estimated)

110,000

50,000 — 100,814

40,000 — 54,523

30,000

20,000 — 24,927

10,000 — 17,592 · 16,270 · 13,798 · 12,906 · 12,703 · 12,448 · 10,034

0

Sioux Falls · Rapid City · Aberdeen · Watertown · Brookings · Mitchell · Pierre · Yankton · Huron · Vermillion

advantage of 'em. In a small town like this, you'd be through in a year."

But small towns have their disadvantages, too. Often, they can't provide everything their residents need. Mobridge, for instance, which has about four thousand people, has only one women's dress shop. But the clothes are too expensive for some people, so they have to drive two hours to Aberdeen or Pierre to find more options.

Small-town life can be particularly hard on the poor, because

South Dakota's long, empty roads can mean many hours of solitary driving.

they are isolated from the services that can help them. In western South Dakota, people may have to travel a hundred miles or more to register for unemployment benefits. If they have no car, they're out of luck: There are no buses or trains to take them.

The neighborly hospitality that pioneers needed to survive has continued to this day. In South Dakota, people are expected to be friendly and helpful. After bicycling through the state, Bruce Weber was pleased to report, "Drivers going the other way wave from behind the wheel . . . and residents . . . seem to be of a particularly gregarious American stripe."

HITTING THE ROAD

South Dakotans love to drive. A motorcyclist races down the twisted roads through the Black Hills. A lone pick-up cruises the rolling plains of the northwest. A businessman is so used to the empty stretches of a straight-as-an-arrow highway that he reads a newspaper while he's driving! For all three, South Dakota's deserted roads offer pleasant relaxation. "Among the simple pleasures of Dakota is driving where there's no traffic," wrote Kathleen Norris, recalling the evening she drove two hundred miles from Rapid City to Lemmon and saw fewer than fifteen cars but more than one hundred antelope.

But driving in South Dakota has its problems: You are in the world of small towns, a world where businesses close in the evening and people go home to their families. Late-night gas stations are few and far between, sometimes as much as two hundred miles apart. The first piece of advice given to any traveler to South Dakota is to fill up your tank whenever you can.

One thing all South Dakotans seem to love is sports. "That's pretty much all anyone around here does," said one Aberdeen woman. They play basketball, baseball, and football with a passion. Hunting and fishing are ways of life. At various times of the year,

HARLEYS IN THE HILLS

West River people love motorcycles. It is not uncommon to see motorcycle gangs of the nicest-looking middle-aged couples, complete with headsets so they can talk to each other. There's something about the landscape that makes people want to get on their bikes and roar off into the sunset.

That roar is loudest in the small town of Sturgis, just on the edge of the Black Hills. Every August, hundreds of thousands of people on Harley Davidsons converge on Sturgis for the world's largest motorcycle rally. During that week they hold drag races, hill climbs, road tours, and motorcycle rodeos. They also enjoy rock concerts and admire each other's bikes. Basically, it's a week-long party. If you want a motel room or don't like noise, stay far away. If you ever fall in love with motorcycles, though, you might find yourself in Sturgis.

South Dakotans are avid hunters and fishermen.

hunters stalk pheasants, grouse, geese, ducks, deer, and antelope. From huge Lake Oahe to a tiny stream in the Black Hills, fishermen wait for a bite from walleyes, catfish, trout, or sturgeon.

CELEBRATING THE PAST

South Dakota's population is overwhelmingly white. About 91.6 percent of the population trace their origins to Europe. American Indians are the next largest group, making up about 7.3 percent of the population. There is also a smattering of blacks, Asians, and

ETHNIC SOUTH DAKOTA

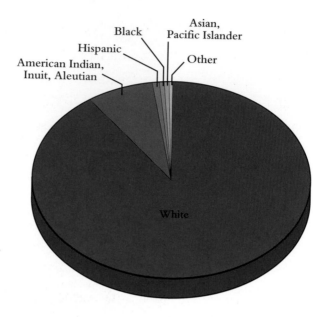

Hispanics. Although many of the pioneers were foreigners—in 1920, 28 percent of South Dakota's population had been born abroad—today only a few immigrants trickle in. In 1993, for example, only 543 immigrants settled in South Dakota.

Germans, Swedes, Norwegians, and many others once came in droves. Some ended up in small towns dominated by their own ethnic group. Today these places celebrate their heritage with festivals during the summer. For instance, each June thousands of people pour into Tabor, a tiny town of four hundred, to enjoy Czech Days. During the two-day celebration, they dance the polka, eat tarts called *kolaches*, and recall what they can of the language spoken by their immigrant parents and grandparents.

Many other towns have festivals and rodeos celebrating their pioneer or Wild West heritage. Every year, De Smet holds the Laura Ingalls Wilder Pageant, which features demonstrations of pioneer skills such as quilting and butter churning, as well as a performance that recreates events from her books. "We feel we're trying to preserve the history and authenticity of Laura Ingalls Wilder," said Donna Bierschbach, who is in charge of publicity for the pageant.

The various Indian reservations throughout the state host annual powwows featuring traditional dancing, crafts, and food.

In Tabor, children celebrate their heritage during Czech Days.

Native Americans keep their traditions alive at powwows, which often feature colorful dancing exhibitions.

Schools on Indian reservations once taught only about white culture, but now they teach Indian students about their traditional culture. Here, students at Crow Creek Tribal School dry buffalo meat.

INDIAN TACOS

South Dakotans love straightforward, all-American food: hamburgers, steak, eggs. But one interesting variation that has grown popular in recent years is the Indian taco. It combines a traditional Indian dish called frybread with the regular ingredients of a taco to create a quick, filling, and delicious meal. Have an adult help you with this recipe.

1½ pounds hamburger
salt
pepper
½ pound cheddar cheese
3 medium tomatoes
1 small head of lettuce
2½ cups flour
½ teaspoon salt
1 teaspoon baking powder
½ teaspoon sugar
1 cup warm milk
3 teaspoons vegetable oil
1 pint sour cream

In a large frying pan, brown hamburger until thoroughly cooked. Add a dash of salt and pepper. Grate the cheese and chop the lettuce and tomatoes.

To make frybread, combine remaining dry ingredients. Add warm milk and 1 teaspoon oil and mix into dough. Divide and shape dough into eight flat pancakes. Heat remaining oil over medium heat. Fry dough in oil until brown and crispy.

On each hot frybread put some hamburger, cheese, lettuce, tomato, and a dollop of sour cream. Eat with a fork. Enjoy.

HERO OR VILLAIN?

After Kevin Costner directed and starred in the film *Dances With Wolves*, many Lakotas considered him a hero. The movie respectfully depicted the lives of the Lakotas before the whites overran them, and it made many Sioux proud.

But now some Sioux feel betrayed by Costner. The actor is building a resort in the Black Hills. Part of it will be on National Forest land that he exchanged for property he owned in Spearfish Canyon. In 1980, the Supreme Court awarded the Sioux more than $100 million for having the Black Hills stolen from them. But the Sioux turned it down. Instead, they want the National Forest land in the Black Hills. They believe that until the issue is settled, none of this land should be traded.

Some Lakotas were surprised that Costner, having made such a sensitive movie about their culture, would turn his back on them. "After the movie, I thought he was pretty cool," says a Lakota named Joe Pulliam. "But now, it seems like he's just another white guy coming here to take what he can get."

Still, many Lakotas give Costner the benefit of the doubt. Doris Leader Charge, who taught Costner the Lakota language for his role in the film, says that by "making a movie that told people all over the world that the Lakota people still live—will always live," Costner has done enough to make him loved by the Sioux for all time.

These events preserve and celebrate Native American culture and are enjoyed by Indians and non-Indians alike.

After suffering so many years of attack, the Lakotas are now doing everything they can to preserve their culture—to maintain the old ways and to remember who they are. Some of this knowledge is passed on at the many tribal colleges that have recently sprung up on reservations. "This is one of the most wonderful revolutions in Indian Country, the right to educate on our own terms," explains Dr. David Gipp of the American Indian Higher Education Committee. At Sinte Gleska University on the Rosebud reservation, in the southern part of the state, all of the students have to study the Lakota language. This is as different as can be from the old government boarding schools, where children were forbidden to speak their native languages and were taught that their culture was inferior.

Guy Dull Knife Jr., who grew up on Pine Ridge, believes that it is necessary for the Lakota to function in the white world *and* to maintain their own traditions. He said, "If we are to make it as a people, our children must know about computers and the Eagle Dance. They must know the value of earning a living and about our traditional relationship with the earth. They need to know how to read and write and balance a checkbook, but they must also know who they are and where they came from. It is our job to teach them these things, just like our fathers before us. Then it will be up to them to help their children learn the ways of both the white world and the Indian world."

5 CREAM OF THE CROP

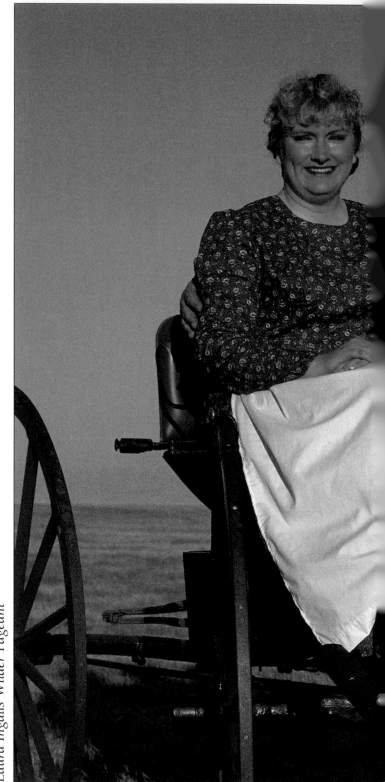

Laura Ingalls Wilder Pageant

Though small in population, South Dakota has produced its fair share of achievers in every field. Whether they made their name in politics, sports, entertainment, or art, these South Dakotans relied on their friendliness and hard work, along with their talent, to take them to the top.

A MAN YOU CAN TRUST

Television networks have frequently looked to America's heartland when hiring broadcasters. People from the center of the nation often come across as all-American—open, honest, friendly, and trustworthy. And they have the neutral accents that television demands. Thus, such South Dakotans as sportscaster Pat O'Brien and *Entertainment Tonight* anchor Mary Hart have become successful. But few names loom as large in the world of television journalism as that of Tom Brokaw, another native South Dakotan.

Brokaw attributes his obsession with current events to growing up in South Dakota. "One of the advantages of a South Dakota childhood is that there is so little around you intellectually that you reach out for broader sources of material," Brokaw once explained. "I was always aware of what was going on in New York or other power centers. . . . I was known as the town talker. I was always involved in whatever arguments were going."

Television newsman Tom Brokaw has been called "the quintessential nice guy."

Like many South Dakota achievers, Brokaw knew what he wanted early and started doing it when he was very young. At fifteen, he got a job after school as a radio announcer. He worked his way through college as a reporter for various radio stations. After graduation, his efforts paid off as he quickly rose through the ranks of television journalism, becoming NBC's White House correspondent, then anchor of the *Today* show, and finally host of the *NBC Nightly News*.

Many people believe Brokaw achieved this fairly quickly because of his wholesomeness and believability. He comes across as comfortable, relaxed, and unfailingly polite, yet he asks the tough questions and avoids fluff. To Brokaw's fans, he is the perfect example of what is best about South Dakotans.

RAGS TO RICHES

Newspaper giant Al Neuharth's life is reminiscent of the desperate struggles of the pioneers. It is a story of poverty, hard work, throwing caution to the wind, and fighting for everything.

Al was born in Eureka, not far from the North Dakota border. Before he was two years old, his father died from injuries in a farm accident. The family struggled by on his mother's meager earnings from cleaning houses, washing dishes, and taking in other people's laundry. Al and his older brother were expected to contribute, as well. So when Al was ten, he got his first paying job, a paper route

Newspaper mogul Al Neuharth once said, "I soaked up my widowed mother's winning ways: You have to struggle to survive. Then strive to succeed. And live to enjoy. Because of her, I often outdid myself."

that earned him twelve cents a week. At thirteen, he was working at a butcher shop, and he later worked at a drug-store soda fountain. No matter where he was, he watched people, learning what he could from them.

At twenty-eight he launched his own newspaper, *SoDak Sports*, a statewide weekly devoted entirely to sports. Although the paper sold a lot of copies, it was a financial disaster and died after a couple of years. Rather than hanging around South Dakota feeling sorry for himself, Neuharth ran off to Florida. There he became a reporter for the *Miami Herald*. Using his feistiness and management skills, he quickly worked his way up through the newspaper world. He eventually became chairman and chief executive officer of the Gannett newspaper chain, which owns about a hundred daily newspapers around the country, as well as dozens of radio and television stations and weekly papers.

What Al Neuharth is best known for is founding *USA Today*, the country's first—and only—nationwide general-interest newspaper. *USA Today* changed how newspapers look. It was the first to have a bright, colorful design and lots of charts and graphs. Soon newspapers all around the world were copying *USA Today*, splashing their drab black-and-white dailies with color.

A SIOUX ARTIST

Oscar Howe's life may not be a rags-to-riches story, but it is an inspiring tale. From a childhood of poverty and illness on the Crow Creek Indian Reservation, Howe became probably the most distinguished artist ever to come from South Dakota.

Artist Oscar Howe once said of his work that "every part comes from Indian and not White culture."

A Yanktonai Sioux, Oscar Howe was born on Crow Creek in 1915 into a desperately poor world. He showed an interest in drawing at an early age and was greatly influenced by his grandmother, Fearless Face, who drew Sioux symbols in the dirt for him to copy, symbols that later made their way into his art. Around age ten, Oscar was sent to the boarding school for Indians in Pierre, where he was miserable and lonely. The school insisted that only English be spoken, and he knew only Sioux. His isolation was made worse by a skin disease that gave him sores and another disease that nearly caused him to go blind.

Yet Howe persevered. And he painted. Even before he attended the Sante Fe Indian School in New Mexico, where he received his first formal art training, his paintings had been included in an exhibition of Indian art that traveled throughout the United States and Europe.

Some of Howe's early work, such as the murals that decorate an auditorium in Mobridge, is realistic. But he is much better known for his flowing, abstract, symbolic art that is reminiscent of cubism, a style of modern art that breaks down images into geometric shapes, then groups the images into patterns. Regardless of the style, Howe always used his paintings to reflect his Sioux culture.

Howe's paintings have been shown all over the world, but his work can also be seen throughout South Dakota. He has paintings in the South Dakota Art Museum in Brookings and murals in Mobridge and Mitchell. Howe also taught at the University of South Dakota for more than twenty years. In recognition of his continuous contributions to the state's artistic heritage, in 1960 he was named the state's artist laureate. He died in 1983.

A NATIONAL LEADER

When Tom Daschle was in high school and people asked him what he wanted to do with his life, he would say, "Well, my dream is someday to be a U.S. senator." Daschle not only achieved that dream, but he went on to become the Democratic Party leader in the Senate—one of the most important political positions in the country.

Throughout his life, Daschle always focused on his goal. At South Dakota State University, he was president of the Young Democrats. After college, he worked as a legislative aide to Senator James Abourezk, learning the secrets of how Washington works. Then he decided to go for it.

In 1978, at the tender age of twenty-eight, he ran for a seat in the

U.S. House of Representatives. Daschle and his wife visited forty thousand homes in his effort to win election. It worked—and he was reelected three times. Then in 1986 his childhood dream came true when he was elected to the U.S. Senate.

In both the House and the Senate, Daschle became an expert in agriculture and veterans' affairs—not high-profile issues, but ones he knew mattered to the folks back home. Daschle gained power by using the traits so common to South Dakotans. He became known as someone everybody liked, who could work with the other senators, someone who has a calm, reasonable, and persuasive voice. He is not strident, not out there screaming at the opposition. Instead, in his own friendly, low-key manner, he builds consensus.

Farmers have a friend in Tom Daschle, the Democratic leader in the U.S. Senate. Daschle is known for his quiet persuasiveness.

Laura Ingalls Wilder says she wrote her books because she "wanted children to understand more about the beginnings of things—what it is that made America."

A PIONEER SPIRIT

One of the most popular and beloved children's book authors went to South Dakota on a wagon in 1879. This was Laura Ingalls Wilder, whose family moved to Dakota to homestead. Four of Laura's eight "Little House" books were set in and around De Smet, on the wide-open prairie in the eastern part of the state.

Laura did not set out to be a writer. She was a farmer's wife, proud and busy on the Missouri land, where she and her husband had moved with their daughter, Rose, after facing one too many disasters in South Dakota. It was Rose who grew up to be a writer, a journalist in San Francisco, and she always encouraged her

MOVING WEST

Laura Ingalls Wilder's tales of pioneer life continue to delight new generations of children. In *By the Shores of Silver Lake*, she writes of moving west onto the vast prairie of Dakota Territory, which was then virtually unsettled by whites.

Beyond the Big Sioux there were no more fields, no houses, no people in sight. There really was no road, only a dim wagon trail, and no railroad grade. Here and there Laura glimpsed a little wooden stake, almost hidden in the grasses. Pa said they were surveyors' stakes for the railroad grade that was not started yet.

Laura said to Mary, "This prairie is like an enormous meadow, stretching far away in every direction, to the very edge of the world."

The endless waves of flowery grasses under the cloudless sky gave her a queer feeling. She could not say how she felt. All of them in the wagon, and the wagon and team, and even Pa, seemed small.

All morning Pa drove steadily along the dim wagon track, and nothing changed. The farther they went into the west, the smaller they seemed, and the less they seemed to be going anywhere. The wind blew the grass always with the same endless rippling, the horses' feet and the wheels going over the grass made always the same sound. The jiggling of the board seat was always the same jiggling. Laura thought they might go on forever, yet always be in the same changeless place, that would not even know they were there.

Only the sun moved. Without ever seeming to, the sun moved steadily upward in the sky.

mother to write. So, in her mid-forties, Laura began writing newspaper columns about farm life. She was particularly expert on the subject of poultry. Gradually she wrote more and more for newspapers and magazines around Missouri.

But what Rose had always loved were her mother's stories of her pioneer childhood. Not until 1930, when Laura was sixty-three, did she sit down to write these stories. So much had changed since her childhood. Now there were automobiles and airplanes, telephones and radios. But when she was little, Laura had often lived in one-room shacks, with no electricity, no nothing. Everything her family needed they made themselves. Back then, the west was still truly wild, the thick forests and endless prairie untrammeled by settlers with their saws and plows. Laura thought it was important that people remember what it was to be a pioneer.

In 1932, when Laura was sixty-five, her first book, *Little House in the Big Woods*, was published. It was an instant hit. Over the next eleven years, seven more books followed, telling of the trials and the triumphs, the fun and games, of one spunky little tomboy and her family as they traveled about the frontier. Laura's books have become classics not only because of the lively way they recreate that world, but also because they embody the integrity, honesty, and hard work that was the true pioneer spirit.

6 FREEWAYS AND BYWAYS

For many people, South Dakota is nothing but one long, straight freeway ride to the Badlands and the Black Hills. But if you take the time to get off the freeway and onto the lonely highways and byways, you will discover some fascinating places and the friendliest of people.

EASTERN SOUTH DAKOTA

In Vermillion, in the extreme southeastern corner of South Dakota, is the Shrine to Music Museum, one of the best museums of musical instruments in the world. Ask the woman at the information desk why this collection—rivaled only by those in such cultural centers as Vienna and Berlin—is here, in a place that many people would call the middle of nowhere, and she laughs, nods her head, and says, "That's what everybody wants to know." The museum began as the property of one very enthusiastic band teacher named Arne B. Larson, who collected more than twenty-five hundred instruments, some of them magnificent antiques, others beat-up trash. He donated the collection to the University of South Dakota. The museum opened in 1973, and the collection has continued to grow ever since.

As visitors stroll the exhibits, they often stop and marvel at an exquisite violin by Antonio Stradivari, the greatest violin maker in history. This beautiful instrument is considered by many to be the finest violin made before 1700. There is also a guitar that he made, one of the only two surviving Stradivari guitars in the world. The collection has examples of instruments from different periods, so you can see how a guitar came to look like a guitar and a saxophone like a saxophone. It also contains fascinating instruments from every corner of the globe. For instance, there is the ud, the great instrument of Arab classical music, which looks something like a mandolin with eleven strings.

For fans of Laura Ingalls Wilder's "Little House" books, De Smet is a must-see. It is the real "little town on the prairie," where Laura's family moved in 1879. The books *By the Shores of Silver Lake, The Long Winter, Little Town on the Prairie,* and *These Happy Golden Years* all take place in and around De Smet. Many Ingalls artifacts remain in the town. You can tour the town's oldest building, the Surveyors' House, where the family spent the winter in *By the Shores of Silver Lake*. The house that Pa built in 1887 is also open to visitors. Although Laura had already married by then, Ma, Pa, and Mary lived out their lives there, and the house contains items that belonged to all the Ingallses, including Laura and her only child, Rose. On the site of the Ingalls homestead, the five cottonwood trees that Pa planted in honor of his wife and four daughters, still stand. De Smet Cemetery contains the graves of all the Ingalls family except Laura, Almonzo, and Rose, as well as graves of other people mentioned in the books.

Mitchell is home to one of the state's oddest tourist attractions, the Corn Palace. The building gets its name from the murals that cover its exterior—murals made of corn. Every September, the

Fans of Laura Ingalls Wilder's books enjoy a visit to the Ingalls homestead.

Thousands of bushels of corn and grass are required to create the murals on the Corn Palace, which has been called "the world's largest bird-feeder."

town celebrates Corn Palace Week, when the previous year's murals are removed and new ones are put up. Inside the building some of the best works are on permanent display. These were created by the Sioux artist Oscar Howe, who designed the Corn Palace murals from 1948 to 1971.

The original structure was built in 1892 to help convince people that eastern South Dakota was a fertile wonderland and a great place to live. Over time, the building was expanded and

embellished. It was given brightly colored towers and minarets, making it look like something out of Disneyland. At first the building was used for agricultural exhibitions. Later, big band concerts were often held there. Today, apart from hosting tourists, it is where local basketball games are played.

Mitchell thrives on the tourists who make it their one stop off of the interstate on the way to the Black Hills. The corn theme is everywhere. You know you're near the Corn Palace, and the center of town, when you see lampposts festooned with corn cobs. Locals seem somewhat bemused by their town's unusual claim to fame. Ask the people who work in the palace's giant gift shop what they think of it, and more likely than not, they will roll their eyes. One young woman said, "It's no big deal. It's just corn. We see it every day. It's where we play our basketball games. Other people come and say 'Wow,' but some people think it's dumb."

CENTRAL SOUTH DAKOTA

Way off the interstate, not far from the North Dakota border, is Mobridge, a town that doesn't get many tourists but is well worth the visit. Just outside of town is the grave of the great Sioux leader Sitting Bull. In 1890, Sitting Bull was killed by government agents just outside his cabin in South Dakota. His body was taken to Fort Yates in North Dakota and unceremoniously buried. In 1953, some of his descendants dug up the bones and reburied them near Mobridge, in Sitting Bull's home territory.

Today the site is marked by a large granite bust sculpted by Korczak Ziolkowski, the same artist who began work on the Crazy

The great Sioux leader Sitting Bull is buried near Mobridge. When government agents pressured him to sell the Black Hills, he responded, "I do not want to sell any land to the government." Picking up a bit of dust, he declared, "Not even as much as this."

Horse memorial in the Black Hills. Chances are, if you visit the grave you will be the only one there, for it is far off the beaten path. But somehow the lonely isolation seems appropriate. If you go in early summer, the surrounding grassland is covered with yellow flowers, and you can sit alone and seem to hear the ancient, sorrowful voices in the steady wind.

Mobridge is also proud of its Scherr-Howe Auditorium. Ten murals by Oscar Howe adorn the inside. During the Great Depression in the 1930s, the federal government established the Works Project Administration to create jobs for people in all lines of work, including artists and writers. Howe was hired to paint the murals in the auditorium. He completed the job in about six weeks for the regular WPA wage of sixty dollars per month. The murals depict the history and everyday life of the Indians in the area and are painted with great pride, dignity, and humanity.

About a hundred miles south of Mobridge is Pierre, the state capital. The city boasts an attractive capitol, complete with marble staircases, mosaic floors, and a shimmering dome. But Pierre's most interesting site is the Cultural Heritage Center, the state historical museum. It includes an excellent exhibit on the ways of life of the plains Indians, including a full-sized tepee, beautiful artifacts, and videos of Indians talking in both Lakota and English about their culture. There are also entertaining displays about the settlers who moved into South Dakota. Historical reconstructions such as a sod house makes clear the hardships suffered by the pioneers.

THE BADLANDS

Perhaps the outstanding attraction in South Dakota is Badlands National Park. With its unearthly spires, gullies, and ridges of ever-changing hues, it is truly a national treasure. At midday, the bright sunshine washes out some of the color in the hills. But in the mornings and evenings, when the light is soft, the greens, reds, oranges, and purples really come to life.

Apart from the main drive that provides numerous places to pull off, sit, and enjoy the fascinating landscape, the park has many hiking trails out into the moonscape. Park rangers offer many interesting programs on the park's geology and animal life, as well as occasional stargazing tours. There are so few buildings in the area that there is no light pollution, so the night sky is truly dark and spectacular, with its fantastic view of millions of stars. An evening in the absolute darkness of the Badlands is not to be missed.

Badlands National Park offers breathtaking views of the surrounding prairies.

FREE ICE WATER

There are a lot of tourist traps in South Dakota and a lot of billboards on the freeway from Sioux Falls to the Black Hills. But there is only one tourist trap that is famous because of its billboards—Wall Drug.

In 1931 Ted and Dorothy Hustead bought the drugstore in the tiny town of Wall, just on the outskirts of the Badlands. This was long before air conditioning, and one scorching South Dakota day, Dorothy realized that the tourists driving from the Badlands to the Black Hills were probably hot and thirsty. So the Husteads put up signs advertising free ice water at Wall Drug. Sure enough, it worked. They attracted plenty of new customers.

The signs multiplied, informing drivers exactly how many miles they were from Wall Drug. These signs became legend and turned up all over the world. From Italy to India to the Arctic Circle, no matter where you were you might suddenly find out how far it was to that small town in South Dakota.

Today, Wall Drug has endless signs on roads heading toward the town, and when you're past it a lot of signs inform you that you missed it. There are signs on freeways, on highways, and on byways. There are more than three thousand Wall Drug signs all over the nation.

Wall Drug has taken over most of the town of Wall. It has become more of a mall than a drugstore, with forty little shops that sell everything from donuts to boots, and an awful lot of tacky souvenirs in between. On a hot summer day, twenty thousand people pass through Wall Drug, looking for ice water.

The southern part of the park, which is much less visited than its northern counterpart, is actually in the Pine Ridge Indian Reservation. The reservation itself offers a heart-wrenching departure from the prepackaged tourism of much of South Dakota. Driving south into Pine Ridge, you enter Shannon County, the poorest county in the nation. The roads become rougher, filled with potholes. The ramshackle houses are few and far between. Every now and then you pass through a small town, which basically consists of a little store and a cafe. The dry and desolate landscape is a reminder that Indian reservations always ended up on the worst land, the land that was of no use to the white men.

Down the road from the town of Porcupine, near a junction not far from the town of Wounded Knee, is a historical marker that tells about the Wounded Knee Massacre. On a nearby hill stand a grave-yard and a memorial to those who died at the battle. Up on that hill, there is no noise but the sound of the relentless wind and a very occasional passing car. Looking around from the solitude of the graveyard at the surrounding hills and valleys, it is easy to imagine the day, a little over a hundred years ago, when the bleeding bodies of men, women, and children lay in the snow. There are no souvenir stands at Wounded Knee, no guided tours, no place to buy a hot dog or an ice cream cone. Its bleak sadness makes it the most moving site in all the state.

In Pine Ridge, the largest town on the reservation, there is another interesting site. The Heritage Center at Red Cloud Indian School has a fine collection of Native American art, including painting, sculpture, and traditional crafts such as beadwork and porcupine quillwork. Every year, the center hosts an art show by Indian artists from all over the United States, the largest such show in the country.

At this remote spot on Pine Ridge Indian Reservation, the Sioux practice an ancient ritual called the Sun Dance, which the U.S. government banned for nearly a century.

THE BLACK HILLS

To many tourists, a vacation in South Dakota means a trip to the Black Hills. The hills cover a relatively small area but are jam-packed with historical sites, fun activities, and natural beauty. Even the roads are tourist attractions. They were built to lure visitors with their magnificent vistas and scenery. The roads through the craggy hills are so winding (some even have full loop-de-loop "pigtail" bridges) that driving is very slow going. The route of the most famous of these, the Iron Mountain Road, was laid out by Peter Norbeck, a former South Dakota governor and senator, who loved the Black Hills more than anywhere else. When people objected to its roundabout route, Norbeck replied, "This is not a commercial highway, it's a scenic road. To do the scenery half-justice, people should drive twenty mph or under; to do it full justice, they should get out and walk!"

Undoubtedly the most famous site in the Black Hills is Mount Rushmore. In the early 1920s, historian Doane Robinson had an idea. He thought it would be great to honor legendary western heroes, such as Lewis and Clark, Buffalo Bill Cody, and a Sioux warrior, by carving a huge sculpture in the Black Hills. But after sculptor Gutzon Borglum took the job, he informed Robinson that his subjects would be national heroes, not western ones. So now, peering out placidly from the side of the mountain are George Washington, Thomas Jefferson, Theodore Roosevelt, and Abraham Lincoln.

Upon first seeing Mount Rushmore, many people are surprised by how small it looks. But don't be fooled. It's actually huge.

Driving through the Black Hills is slow going, especially on the pigtail bridges.

Gutzon Borglum, the sculptor who created Mount Rushmore, once said, "American art ought to be monumental, in keeping with American life."

George Washington's face is 60 feet tall. If he had a body, he would be 465 feet tall.

Down the road a way, another mountain is being carved that dwarfs Mount Rushmore. This eventually will be a giant sculpture of Crazy Horse sitting on his steed and pointing into the distance. Crazy Horse was a great Lakota warrior who was never defeated in battle, never photographed, never wore white men's clothes or accepted any part of white culture. Work on the sculpture began in 1946. Crazy Horse's face, which is 87½ feet tall, will be finished in 1998. Also visible are much of the horse's head and Crazy Horse's outstretched arm. When complete, the sculpture will be more than 600 feet long and 563 feet tall, carved three-dimensionally so you can look at it from all sides.

The Black Hills are famous for their abundance of caves. The hills were formed when molten rock from deep inside the earth forced its way upward through a layer of limestone. This left cracks in the limestone. Water running through these cracks gradually wore away the rock and over millions of years created the vast cave mazes in the hills. The most famous is Wind Cave National Park. Wind Cave is renowned for its delicate formations, such as box-work—a paper-thin formation that looks like a honeycomb, is easily broken, and is found in only one other cave in the world. Other beautiful formations that can be seen on tours of Wind Cave are frostwork, which looks like a tiny bush covered with frost, and popcorn, which looks just like its name.

One of the biggest attractions in the Black Hills is the Mammoth Site. Mammoths were giant creatures that looked something like elephants: each of them ate seven hundred pounds of grass every

The sculpture of Crazy Horse will be the largest sculpture in the world; all four heads on Mount Rushmore would fit inside the warrior's head.

Wind Cave is known for its delicate formations, such as this aragonite bush.

day. About twenty-six thousand years ago, there was a pond where the site is now located. Mammoths went there for a dip, but the sides of the pond were too steep and slippery for them to get back out. Over time the watering hole disappeared, but the mammoth skeletons remained. In 1974, while the site was being leveled to build a house, a worker came across a glimmering white, seven-foot-long tusk. Work on the housing project stopped. As geologists began excavating the site, they found more and more bones. Rather than carting them all off to a museum or laboratory, they decided to leave most of the bones and tusks where they lay and just

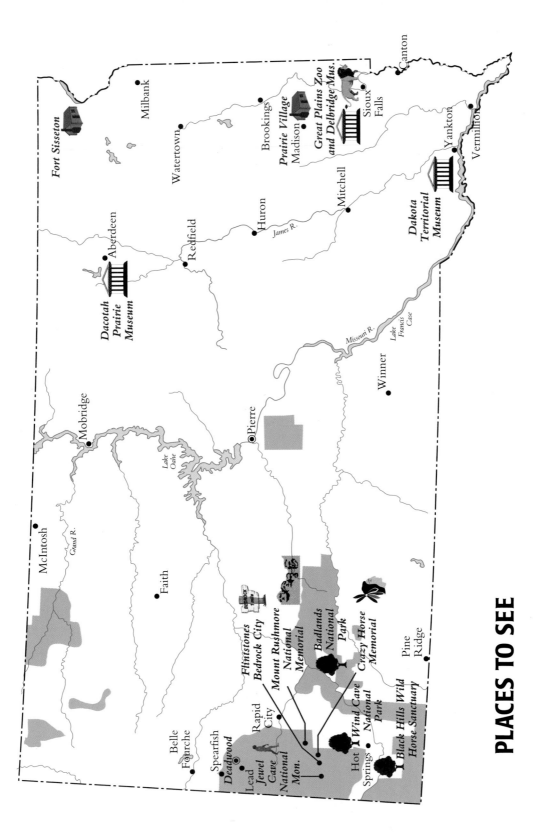

PLACES TO SEE

Fort Sisseton

Milbank

Watertown

Brookings

Prairie Village Madison

Great Plains Zoo and Delbridge Mus.

Sioux Falls

Yankton

Vermillion

Dacotah Prairie Museum

Aberdeen

Redfield

Huron

James R.

Mitchell

Dakota Territorial Museum

Lake Francis Case

Missouri R.

Winner

Mobridge

Lake Oahe

Pierre

McIntosh

Grand R.

Faith

Flintstones Bedrock City

Mount Rushmore National Memorial

Badlands National Park

Crazy Horse Memorial

Pine Ridge

Belle Fourche

Spearfish

Deadwood

Lead

Jewel Cave National Mon.

Rapid City

Hot Springs

Wind Cave National Park

Black Hills Wild Horse Sanctuary

Canton

remove the dirt from around them. This means that when you visit the site, not only can you see the bones as they were found, but you can also sometimes see paleontologists at work, carefully digging, sifting, and scratching the dirt. To date, they have uncovered the remains of fifty mammoths, making it the largest find of this kind anywhere in the world. And they are nowhere near the bottom of the hole yet.

Despite all these attractions, probably the greatest sites in the Black Hills are the hills themselves—their rocky peaks, dark forests, and clear streams—and the abundant wildlife. Driving through the hills, you will likely see white-tail deer, pronghorns, mule deer, and prairie dogs. If you're lucky, you will see coyote and bighorn sheep. And you will most definitely see buffalo.

Both Wind Cave National Park and Custer State Park have herds of the magnificent creatures roaming free. You will see old buffalo and calves, males and females, grazing, rolling around on their backs, or just standing stock still, seeming to stare at you. Some will be off in the distance, but many will be right outside the window of your car. It's virtually impossible to drive through these parks without seeing a buffalo. In fact, you will see so many that soon you will not even want to bother to stop and take a picture. Of course, when a herd of the giant beasts park themselves in the road without the least concern for your desire to get back to town for dinner, there's nothing to do but wait. In South Dakota, that's what passes for a traffic jam.

In Custer State Park, buffalo again roam free.

THE FLAG: The flag was adopted in 1992. The state seal lies at the center and is encircled by a yellow sunburst against a blue background. The words "South Dakota The Mount Rushmore State" are printed around the sunburst.

THE SEAL: The border reads "State of South Dakota, Great Seal, 1889." The picture inside the circle shows the elements of the state's economy. A farmer plows in the foreground. A steamboat, a smelter furnace, and grazing cattle in the background represent trade, industry, and agriculture, The state motto, "Under God the People Rule," is written at the top of the picture.

STATE SURVEY

Statehood: November 2, 1889

Origin of Name: South Dakota comes from the Sioux Indians who called themselves Dakota or Lakota, meaning "friends" or "allies."

Nickname: The Mount Rushmore State, The Sunshine State, Coyote State

Capital: Pierre

Ring-necked pheasant

Motto: Under God the People Rule

Bird: Ring-necked pheasant

Animal: Coyote

Fish: Walleye

Flower: American pasqueflower

Pasqueflower

Tree: Black Hills spruce

Mineral: Rose quartz

Gem: Fairburn agate

Insect: Honeybee

Musical instrument: Fiddle

Soil: Houdek soil

Grass: Western wheat grass

Colors: Blue and gold

GEOGRAPHY

Highest Point: Harney Peak, 7,242 feet

Lowest Point: Big Stone Lake, 962 feet

Area: 77,122 square miles

Greatest Distance, North to South: 237 miles

Greatest Distance, East to West: 383 miles

Bordering States: Montana and Wyoming to the west, North Dakota to the north, Minnesota and Iowa to the east, Nebraska to the south

Hottest Recorded Temperature: 120°F at Gannvalley on July 5, 1936

Coldest Recorded Temperature: −58°F at McIntosh on February 17, 1936

Average Annual Precipitation: 18 inches

Major Rivers: Bad, Big Sioux, Cheyenne, Grand, James, Little Missouri, Missouri, Vermillion, White

Major Lakes: Francis Case, Oahe, Sharpe

Trees: ash, cottonwood, juniper, oak, pines, spruces

Wild Plants: American pasqueflower, black-eyed Susan, cactus, forget-me-not, goldenrod, lady-slipper, larkspur, mariposa lily, sunflower, wild orange geranium

HAIL! SOUTH DAKOTA

One hundred fifty-eight songs were submitted in a statewide contest for an official state song. The judges chose "Hail! South Dakota," composed by Deecort Hammitt, director of the Alcester municipal band. The song was officially adopted on March 5, 1943.

Words & Music by Deecort Hammitt

Hail! South Da - ko - ta, A great state of the land.

Health, wealth and beau - ty, That's what makes her grand.

She has her Black Hills, And mines with gold so rare,

And with her scen - 'ry No state can com - pare.

Animals: buffalo, bighorn sheep, coyote, elk, mule deer, pronghorn antelope, Rocky Mountain goat, white-tailed deer

Birds: Hungarian partridge, prairie chicken, ring-necked pheasant, sage grouse, sharp-tailed grouse, wild turkey

Fish: bass, bluegill, catfish, crappie, northern pike, paddlefish, perch, sauger, sturgeon, trout (brook, brown, rainbow), walleyed pike

Endangered Animals: American burying beetle, bald eagle, banded killfish, blackfooted ferret, blacknose shiner, Blanding's turtle, central mudminnow, Eskimo curlew, finescale dace, gray wolf, interior least tern, lined snake, pallid sturgeon, peregrine falcon, whooping crane

Endangered Plants: none endangered; one threatened: western prairie fringed orchid

Blanding's turtle

TIMELINE

South Dakota History

A.D. **500** Mound Builders appear along Big Sioux River

1600s Arikara tribe settle along Missouri River

1682 René-Robert Cavelier, sieur de La Salle, claimed for France all land drained by the Mississippi River, including area that became South Dakota

1743 François La Verendrye and Louis-Joseph La Verendrye become first white explorers to reach South Dakota region

1750–1790 Sioux drive Arikara up Missouri River

1780 Pierre Dorion is first European settler in South Dakota

1803 United States acquires South Dakota as part of Louisiana Purchase

1804, 1806 Meriweather Lewis and William Clark travel through South Dakota on their trek to the Pacific Northwest

1817 Joseph La Framboise establishes first permanent settlement in South Dakota

1861 Congress creates Dakota Territory, consisting of present-day North and South Dakota and much of Montana and Wyoming

1862 Homestead Act passed to encourage settlement of western lands

1868 Laramie Treaty ends Red Cloud's War and establishes Great Sioux Reservation, which includes Black Hills and other land as far as western Wyoming

1874 U.S. government violates treaty by sending General Custer to investigate reports of gold in Black Hills; gold rush and Indian uprisings begin

1876 Indians give up claims to Black Hills

1876 Custer and his troops defeated at the Battle of Little Bighorn

1889 South Dakota becomes fortieth state

1890 Last major confrontation between U.S. Army and Indians takes place with massacre of hundreds of Sioux at Wounded Knee Creek on Pine Ridge Indian Reservation

1890 Pierre becomes state capital

1927 Work on Mount Rushmore begins

1930s Severe drought (Dust Bowl) in South Dakota causing economic hardship

1944 Congress authorizes construction of four hydroelectric dams on Missouri River to provide electric power, flood control, and irrigation

1960s United States places missile sites in state

1972 South Dakota Senator George McGovern nominated as Democratic presidential candidate

1973 Native American group occupies Wounded Knee village for 71 days

1980 U.S. Supreme Court orders state to pay South Dakota Indian nations for land seized in 1877

1991–1994 United States removes missiles from state as part of international nuclear disarmament agreement

1993 Flooding causes severe crop damage estimated at more than $725 million

ECONOMY

Agricultural Products: cattle, corn, hay, hogs, oats, rye, sorghum, soybeans, sunflowers, wheat

Manufactured Products: clothing, electric and electronic equipment, food and food products, glass products, machinery

Sunflowers

Natural Resources: beryl, feldspar, gold, mica, Ponderosa pine, Portland cement, silver, uranium

Business and Trade: communication, electric power, transportation, communication

CALENDAR OF CELEBRATIONS

Volksmarch During the first weekend of June, the top of Thunderhead Mountain is open to the public. Tourists can view up close the work in progress on the Crazy Horse Memorial that honors Crazy Horse and all American Indians. When completed (scheduled for 1998), it will be 563 feet high and 641 feet long, and it will be the largest sculpture in the world.

Fort Sisseton Historical Festival The first weekend of June, Fort Sisseton State Park hosts this festival that celebrates pioneer days. It includes cavalry and infantry drills, square dancing, melodrama, frontier crafts, costume ball, draft horse pull, and a Dutch oven bake-off.

Cavalry drill

Laura Ingalls Wilder Pageant For three weekends (last week of June and first two weeks of July), this event near De Smet celebrates through drama the life and times of the famed children's author. Visitors can also enjoy wagon rides and other entertainment and tour the site of the Ingalls homestead.

Black Hills Passion Play Each week during June, July, and August professional actors and residents re-enact a Passion Play (religious drama) that dates back more than 700 years to Lunen, Germany, where monks performed the play during Easter week. You can also take a backstage tour of the amphitheater located in Spearfish.

Black Hills Roundup Cowboy days live on at the Roundup. Since 1918, residents and visitors in Belle Fourche have celebrated the Fourth of July with three days of parades and rodeo events, such as bucking contests and steer-roping.

Gold Discovery Days For two days in late July, the town of Custer celebrates the discovery of gold on French Creek in 1874. The event includes rodeos, Indian dances, and a street carnival. There is also a pageant re-enacting the Custer expedition, the gold rush, Old West lifestyles, and effects of United States expansion on the Indian population.

Days of '76 Every August, Deadwood re-enacts its history as a gold rush boom town that attracted thousands of gold seekers as well as gunfighters and gamblers such as Wild Bill Hickok, Calamity Jane, Doc Holliday, and Wyatt Earp. The town celebrates those wild days with a rodeo, a pageant, re-enactments of historical events, and games. In addition there is a three-mile-long parade of ox teams, covered wagons, buggies, stagecoaches, and pack mules.

Steam Threshing Jamboree Steam powers this annual August event at Prairie Village, near Madison. You can watch as antique farm machinery, a train, and even a merry-go-round are fired up by steam engines. This celebration of days-gone-by also includes parades, arts and crafts displays, square dancing, tractor pulls, and threshing demonstrations.

Rosebud Sioux Tribal Fair and Powwow Late August brings native tribes together in Rosebud for traditional dances, arts and crafts exhibits, and a buffalo dinner. This powwow, and others held during the summer, keep alive the traditions of the Great Sioux Nation and introduce its culture to visitors.

Black Hills Sawdust Day Timber is one of the Black Hills' major industries, and this is the largest logging event in the region. Lumberjacks show off their skills by competing in tree felling, saw bucking, ax and chain throwing, and wood splitting. It is held in Spearfish on the Saturday after Labor Day.

Corn Palace Festival The Corn Palace was built in 1892 to encourage settlement and prove how productive the soil was. It is decorated inside and outside with thousands of bushels of corn, grain, and grasses. For a week at the end of September, the end of the harvest season, this renowned and historic "palace" brings in name performers and speakers.

STATE STARS

George Lee (Sparky) Anderson (1934–   ),
    former manager of the Cincinnati Reds and

Detroit Tigers, was the first manager to achieve 100 wins in both the American and National Leagues and to manage World Series winners in both leagues. He was born in Bridgewater.

L. Frank Baum (1856–1919), author of the *Wonderful Wizard of Oz* and thirteen other Oz books grew up in the Aberdeen area, and edited and published that city's weekly paper. He also wrote *Father Goose* (1899) and other children's books. He was born in Chittenango, New York.

L. Frank Baum

Gutzon Borglum (1867–1941), the sculptor most famous for his gigantic work at Mount Rushmore, was born in Idaho. Borglum studied art in San Francisco and Paris, where he became friends with the French sculptor Auguste Rodin. He moved to New York in 1901 and became a popular sculptor of portraits and public monuments, including a six-ton marble head of Abraham Lincoln for the U.S. Capitol rotunda. He began work on Mount Rushmore in 1927. He and his crew spent 12 years, using pneumatic drills and dynamite, to carve the likenesses of Presidents Washington, Jefferson, Lincoln, and Theodore Roosevelt. Each head is 60 feet high.

Tom Brokaw (1940–   ), born in Webster, hosted NBC's *Today Show* for six years. He became co-anchor with Roger Mudd of the *NBC Nightly News* in 1981 and its sole anchor in 1983. Brokaw was White House correspondent during the Watergate scandal and President Nixon's resignation.

Martha Jane (Calamity Jane) Burke (1852–1903), born in Missouri, was a frontierswoman, expert rider, and markswoman. She also became a star of Buffalo Bill's Wild West Show. She told stories about being a pony express rider and a scout for General Custer, but it is difficult to know what is fact and what is legend about her life. One legend says she got her nickname because she told men it would be their calamity if they offended her. Dressed in men's clothing, she was a familiar figure in Deadwood. She is buried next to Wild Bill Hickok in the town's Mount Moriah Cemetery.

Crazy Horse (1842?–1877), chief of the Oglala Sioux, participated in Red Cloud's War (1866–68). During the Sioux uprising of 1876–77, he defeated General George Crook at Rosebud Creek in Montana, and eight days later, he helped to defeat General George Custer at the Battle of Little Bighorn. Crazy Horse surrendered to federal troops in May 1877 but was killed several months later, allegedly while trying to escape.

Hallie Flanagan (1890–1969), theater organizer, teacher, and playwright, was born in Redfield. She co-authored *Can You Hear Their Voices*, a play about Arkansas farmers, and headed the Federal Theater Project, which brought live theater to millions of Americans during the Depression in the 1930s.

Gall (1840–1894), a Sioux warrior, fought along with Crazy Horse and Sitting Bull in the Battle of the Little Bighorn, in which General George Custer was killed and his Seventh Cavalry defeated.

Hamlin Garland (1860–1940), a writer, was born in West Salem, Wisconsin; his family homestead

Gall

was in Ordway, South Dakota. His books included *Main-Travelled Roads, Prairie Folks, Rose of Dutcher's Coolly, A Son of the Middle Border, The Book of the American Indian*, and *A Daughter of the Middle Border*, which won a Pulitzer Prize. Garland's works described the frustrations and hardships of pioneering on the Plains.

Hamlin Garland

Alvin H. Hansen (1887–1975), an economist, was born in Viborg. He believed that a depression like that of the 1930s could be prevented by government planning, and he urged greater government spending on roads, hospitals, schools, and housing.

Mary Hart (1951–   ), born in Sioux Falls, is a television talk show host best known for her work on *Entertainment Tonight*.

James Butler (Wild Bill) Hickok (1837–1876), was a legendary Indian fighter and frontier marshall. Born in Illinois, he left his family's farm when he was 18 and traveled west to the Nebraska Territory. He was a federal scout during the Civil War and later toured with Buffalo Bill's Wild West Show. During the Gold Rush of 1876, he moved to Deadwood, where he was killed in a saloon and buried in the town's cemetery, along with other legends of the Wild West, including Calamity Jane.

Hubert Horatio Humphrey Jr. (1911–1978), was born in Wallace and served as the thirty-eighth vice president of the United States (1965–1969). Humphrey worked as a pharmacist before becoming involved in Minnesota politics. He was elected mayor of Minneapolis in 1945 and U.S. Senator in 1948. He served in the senate until 1964 when he was chosen as President Lyndon Johnson's running mate.

He ran for president in 1968 and was narrowly defeated by Richard Nixon. He returned to the senate in 1971 and unsuccessfully sought the Democratic presidential nomination in 1972 and 1976. Humphrey was a strong supporter of civil rights.

Hubert Horatio Humphrey Jr.

Oscar Howe (1915–1983), Yanktonai Sioux artist, was born in Crow Creek. His abstract paintings and murals, displayed throughout the state, depict stories about Indian life and spirituality. He taught at the University of South Dakota, and in 1960, he was named the state's artist laureate.

Oscar Howe

Ernest O. Lawrence (1901–1958), 1939 Nobel Prize winner in physics, was born in Canton. His invention of the cyclotron, which accelerates atomic particles to produce artificial radioactivity, has been important in the fields of nuclear physics and medicine. The element lawrencium is named for him. He was also instrumental in the development of the atomic bomb.

George McGovern (1922–   ), South Dakota's senator for three terms, was born in Avon. He was the Democratic nominee for the U.S. presidency in 1972. He was overwhelmingly defeated by Richard Nixon despite strong support from opponents of the Vietnam War. First elected to the Senate in 1962, he had worked as a professor of history, a U.S. representative, and director of the Food for Peace program. He lost his bid for a fourth U.S. Senate term in 1980.

George McGovern

Allen Neuharth (1924–   ), born in Eureka, founded the newspaper *USA Today* in 1982. He was formerly chairman of Gannett Company Inc., which owns a chain of newspapers.

Red Cloud (1822–1909), born in Nebraska, was head chief of the Oglala Sioux and leader of the Indian resistance during the 1860s, which became known as Red Cloud's War. This war ended with Red Cloud's signing of the Laramie Treaty in 1868. He went to live on a reservation, losing his status as head chief in 1881.

Ole E. Rolvaag (1876–1931) is best known for his realistic writings about Norwegian settlers on the Dakota prairies. Born in Norway, he immigrated to the United States in 1896 and became a citizen in 1908. Two novels that he wrote in his native language were translated into English and combined as *Giants in the Earth*.

Earle Sande (1898–1968), won the Triple Crown of racing in 1930 riding Gallant Fox. Born in Groton, he was a well-accomplished jockey, winning more than 950 races, including the Kentucky Derby three times and the Belmont Stakes five times. He was named to racing's Hall of Fame in 1955.

Sitting Bull (1831–1890) was a great Sioux leader of the Hunkpapa Lakota nation. Born on Grand River, he opposed the surrender of land and mining rights to the United States after gold was discovered in the Black Hills. He fought along with Gall and Crazy Horse at the Battle of Little Bighorn, then fled to Canada. He returned in 1881 and was imprisoned for two years. He then traveled with Buffalo Bill's Wild West Show. Sitting Bull again became active in Indian affairs and was arrested in 1890 for that involvement. He was killed by Indian guards during the disturbance following his arrest.

Sitting Bull

Joseph Ward (1838–1889) was a leader in South Dakota's efforts to become a state and is credited with establishing its public education system. He founded Yankton Academy, which became the first college in the upper Mississippi River valley. Ward was born in New York state.

Laura Ingalls Wilder (1867–1957), born in Wisconsin, lived in De Smet and wrote about growing up on the frontier. Her books included *Little House on the Prairie, On the Banks of Plum Creek, By the Shores of Silver Lake, The Long Winter,* and *Little Town on the Prairie.*

Korczak Ziolkowski (1908–1982), a Polish orphan who grew up in Boston, was the sculptor behind the still-unfinished Crazy Horse Memorial, which will be the largest sculpture in the world—563 feet high and 631 feet wide. After he died, his family continued his work.

TOUR THE STATE

Badlands National Park (near Rapid City) This "moonscape" of canyons, spires, and razor-edged ridges became a national monument in 1939 and a national park in 1978. You can see bison, pronghorn antelope, mule deer, prairie dogs, and Rocky Mountain Bighorn sheep and learn about the wildlife and geology from exhibits, lectures, and other events led by park rangers.

Mammoth Site (Hot Springs) Visit the largest concentration of mammoth bones found in the Western Hemisphere. Take a guided tour of current diggings, learn the history of the site, view the remains of mammoths, giant short-faced bears, and other animals that died there more than 25,000 years ago.

Dinosaur Park (Rapid City) Visitors can see life-size steel and cement models of dinosaurs that once roamed the land that is now South Dakota.

Halley Park (Rapid City) The Sioux Indian Museum & Crafts Center (exhibits of historic and contemporary Native-American crafts) and Minnilusa Pioneer Museum (exhibits of historical items from pioneer days in Dakotas and Black Hills) are both located here.

Thunderhead Underground Falls (Rapid City) This is one of the oldest (1878) gold mining tunnels in the Black Hills. The underground falls are an easy 600-foot walk from the entrance.

Jewel Cave National Monument (near Custer) With more than 70 miles of passageways, this is the second-longest cave system in the country. Take a scenic or historic tour of the monument. If you are older than 16 years and in good condition, you can try spelunking (exploring caves).

Wind Cave National Park (near Custer) The park, established in 1903, is really two parks—one below ground and one at the surface. The park is named for the strong currents that blow in and out of the cave entrance. There are more than 44 miles of underground passages in the park, connecting chambers with names such as Garden of Eden and Blue Grotto. You have a choice of guided tours of various lengths. Above ground are grasslands, forests, and a wildlife preserve. You can also tour the nearby Black Hills.

Crazy Horse Memorial (near Custer) This giant sculpture of the great Sioux chief was carved out of a granite mountain. Sculptor Korczak Ziolkowski worked on it from 1948 until his death in 1982, and members of his family have continued the work. At the base, you can see scale models of the sculpture and exhibits that explain the drilling and blasting process. The Indian Museum of North America is also located here.

Custer State Park (near Hot Springs) One of the world's largest herds of bison roam this 73,000-acre state park. As you drive around the 18-mile Wildlife Loop, watch for the bison as well as mountain goats, Rocky Mountain bighorn sheep, burro, and other creatures. Visitors can fish, swim, ride horses, paddle boats, rent bikes, or camp.

1880 Train (Hill City) Ride along gold-rush era tracks on a train pulled by a steam engine. The two-hour round trip between Hill City and Keystone takes you through scenic national forests and meadows.

1880 Train

Mount Rushmore National Memorial (Keystone) The heads of Presidents Washington, Jefferson, Lincoln, and Theodore Roosevelt are carved on the face of the mountain. Sculptor Borglum had intended to sculpt them to the waist, but he died before completing the work. An orientation center provides information about the memorial and the sculptor's studio features tools, models, paintings, and photographs of the construction process.

National Museum of Woodcarving (Custer) Thousands of woodcarvings are displayed, including works by one of the original Disney animators who created miniature to life-size figures that move and speak.

Mount Moriah Cemetery (Deadwood) Come see the Wild West of legend when you visit the town of Deadwood with its many reminders of the gold rush days. Take a tour of the town and visit Mount Moriah Cemetery, commonly known as "Boot Hill," where legendary figures from the gold rush days are buried.

The Ghosts of Deadwood Gulch Wax Museum (Deadwood) This Museum features more than 70 lifesize wax figures depicting life in the area, from the arrival of the first white people through the Wild West days when Calamity Jane, "Deadwood Dick," Wild Bill Hickok, and other colorful characters gathered here to cash in on the gold rush.

Black Hills Mining Museum (Lead) Exhibits, videos, photographs, and lifesize figures take you back through the development of a mine that has been in operation since 1876. A tour of a pretend underground mine helps you understand the operation of a gold mine. You can even try panning for gold yourself.

Homestake Gold Mines Surface Tours (Lead) Homestake Gold Mine is one of the oldest and largest underground gold mines in the Western Hemisphere. Take a one-hour tour through surface operations. If you've ever wondered how gold is extracted from the earth, watch an audio-visual presentation about the mining and refining of this valuable substance. Visitors also may tour the surface workings of the largest gold mine in operation in the United States.

Fort Sisseton State Park (Sisseton) Fourteen of the fort's brick and stone buildings, built in 1864 as part of the army's frontier post, have been restored. You can also visit other historical exhibits, or if you like outdoor activities, you can hike, picnic, and camp.

Laura Ingalls Wilder Memorial (De Smet) If you are a fan of the *Little House* books, you won't want to miss this memorial to the author. It includes the family home from 1879, a replica of a schoolhouse, a surveyor's house, and other buildings mentioned in her books.

Prairie Village (Madison) Get a feel for pioneer life by spending time at this replica of a pioneer town. It includes 40 restored buildings, including a one-room schoolhouse, theater, cabins, and churches, as well as antique farm equipment, cars, a steam merry-go-round, and steam trains.

Shrine to Music Museum (Vermillion) Music lovers will want to see this collection of more than 3,000 musical instruments. The exhibit of Italian stringed instruments from the sixteenth through eighteenth centuries features a Stradivari violin and a rare Stradivari guitar. Other collections include traditional instruments from America and around the world.

Dakota Territorial Museum (Yankton) This museum of pioneer life includes the restored Dakota Territorial Council Building and replicas of a railroad depot, caboose, rural schoolhouse, dentist's office, general store, saloon, and blacksmith shop.

Oscar Howe Art Center (Mitchell) The work of Sioux artist Oscar Howe is exhibited here, along with other exhibits of Native American art and culture.

The Corn Palace (Mitchell) With its Moorish architecture, this huge and unique building looks as if belongs in Spain. It is decorated inside and outside with murals made from corn, grains, and grasses. Each year 2,000 to 3,000 bushels of the various grains and grasses are used. Decorative panels inside were designed by artist Oscar Howe.

Enchanted World Doll Museum (Mitchell) More than 4,000 dolls are housed in this castle-like museum complete with a moat, drawbridge, and stained glass windows. The dolls are arranged in 400 scenes from fairy tales, nursery rhymes, children's books, and eighteenth and nineteenth century history.

Wounded Knee Historical Site (Pine Ridge) A monument marks the mass grave where 200 Sioux men, women, and children were shot by the U.S. Army.

FUN FACTS

The geographic center of the United States, including Alaska and Hawaii, is located in western South Dakota, about seventeen miles west of Castle Rock.

The town of Sturgis was once a bullwhackers' (wagon drivers') stop on the way to Fort Meade. It was known as Scooptown because soldiers were "scooped"—cleaned out of all their money—by the cigar-smoking Poker Alice and other gamblers.

Want to predict the weather? Wind Cave can be your barometer. When the wind blows out of the cave, it means the barometer is falling. When the wind blows into the cave, the barometer is rising.

The Indian name for the Black Hills is *Paha Sapa*—"hills that are black." Those hills are not really hills; they are domed mountains. And they are not really black—they are dense with dark green trees. The Paha Sapa are older than the Rockies, the Alps, or the Himalayas.

FIND OUT MORE

If you'd like to find out more about South Dakota, look in your library, bookstore, or video store. Here are some titles to ask for:

STATE BOOKS

Sirvaitis, Karen, and Dennis Fradin. *South Dakota*. Minneapolis: Lerner, 1995.

Lepthien, Emilie U. *America the Beautiful: South Dakota*. Chicago: Childrens Press, 1991.

SPECIAL INTEREST BOOKS

Bernatos, Bob. *Sitting Bull: Chief of the Sioux*. New York: Chelsea House, 1992.

Blumberg, Rhoda. *The Incredible Journey of Lewis and Clark*. New York: Lothrop, Lee & Shepard, 1987.

Cavan, Seamus. *Lewis and Clark and the Route to the Pacific*. New York: Chelsea House, 1991.

Dolan, Terrance. *The Teton Sioux Indians*. New York: Chelsea House, 1995.

Faber, Doris. *Calamity Jane: Her Life and Legend*. Boston: Houghton Mifflin, 1992.

Freedman, Russell. *The Life and Death of Crazy Horse*. New York: Holiday House, 1996.

Giff, Particia Reilly. *Laura Ingalls Wilder: Growing Up in the Little House*. New York: Viking Kestral, 1987.

Wilder, Laura Ingalls. *By the Shores of Silver Lake*. New York: HarperCollins, 1971.

———. *Little Town on the Prairie*. New York: HarperCollins, 1971.

———. *The Long Winter*. New York: HarperCollins, 1971.

———. *These Happy Golden Years*. New York: HarperCollins, 1971.

VIDEOS

Dances With Wolves. 181 min. Orion Home Video, 1995. Videocassette.

Mt. Rushmore & the Black Hills of South Dakota. 30 min. Finlay Holiday Films, 1985. Videocassette.

WEBPAGE

On the Internet, you can find the State of South Dakota Home Page, which will have pictures, facts, and suggestions for further research about the state. Go to www.state.sd.us on the World Wide Web.

INDEX

Page numbers for illustrations are in boldface.